INCARCERATION

MY FIVE YEARS AS A POLITICAL PRISONER IN IRAN

Farzaneh Djalalian Asl

First published by Busybird Publishing 2021

Copyright © 2021 Farzaneh Djalalian Asl

ISBN
978-1-922691-23-1 (paperback)
978-1-922691-24-8 (ebook)

The information in this book is based on the author's experiences and opinions. The author and publisher disclaim responsibility for any adverse consequences, which may result from use of the information contained herein. Permission to use any external content has been sought by the author. Any breaches will be rectified in further editions of the book.

Cover design: Busybird Publishing

Layout and typesetting: Busybird Publishing

Busybird Publishing
2/118 Para Road
Montmorency, Victoria
Australia 3094
www.busybird.com.au

I'd like to dedicate this book to my loving family, especially, my late father and my beautiful mother. To their unconditional love for me and my siblings. I was not the only one who suffered five years of injustice. They also suffered a great deal. From the first night that I did not return home to those anxious days and hours they searched the hospitals trying to find me wounded there. To those endless hours searching through the dead bodies in the cemeteries.

My dedication is also to those friends and fellow prisoners who we screamed and fought together for freedom and justice. Those who we spent more than five years in the Evin and then the Ghezel Hesar prison. The support we gave to each other during those tormenting five years, kept us going. Those who lost their live during the protest and those who got executed later in the Prison.

Contents

Acknowledgements   1

Chapter 1   3
     Arrest

Chapter 2   9
     Background on Iran

Chapter 3   17
     My Family and Childhood

Chapter 4   27
     University and Political Involvement

Chapter 5   33
     Evin Prison

Chapter 6   41
     The New Evin Cell

Chapter 7   57
     Relocation to Ghezel Hesar

Chapter 8   61
     Life in Ghezel Hesar

Chapter 9   65
     Transfer to Punishment Ward

Chapter 10   71
     Visitation

Chapter 11   75
     Illness in Prison

Chapter 12   79
    Interrogation

Chapter 13   83
    Release

Chapter 14   89
    First Day of Freedom

Chapter 15   93
    Out of Prison but Not Free

Chapter 16   101
    Escape from Iran

Chapter 17   109
    Ten Months in Turkey

Chapter 18   121
    Finally, Australia!

Acknowledgements

First, I want to thank my late father and my beautiful mum for their endless love for me and my siblings. If it wasn't for them, I might never have survived those five dreadful years. And thanks to my siblings, who supported me in many different ways throughout my journey.

In 2012, I had the pleasure of meeting David Murphy through a friend, Antonette Ziffer. David not only edited my drafts, he was also a welcome support the whole way through my writing. His feedback, his suggestions, his flexibility and his brain storming were a great help. I learned a great deal from him on how to write a memoir and tell the story behind it.

Also, a big thank you to Antonette for her support and introduction.

I am also grateful for my friend, Barbara Denham, who made time to listen while I read parts of the story to get her feedback. Her encouragement and appreciation of my writing lifted my spirits.

Acknowledgements

CHAPTER 1

Arrest

On the morning of 30 Khordad 1360 (the Persian date for 20 June 1981), my friends and I set off to participate in what turned out to be one of the biggest protests in Iran's history. We wanted freedom, democracy and more – all the things that the Khomeini regime had taken away from us.

It was Saturday, the first day of the week in Iran, and as usual I woke up early at about 5:30 am. It was a pleasant morning, with a clear blue sky starting to lighten up. I was a little anxious, even scared, but that didn't deter me from the pursuit of my beliefs. The day before, I had asked my mother to cut my hair short, as summer was with us and since I was wearing a scarf at the time, I would cope more easily with the heat. I didn't know what was waiting for me, but had been subconsciously preparing myself for unexpected events. I knew that I was going to be part of a major demonstration and from what I had seen from this fanatical Islamic government, being nervous was understandable.

My anxiety was justified, as for the previous couple of years since the revolution, horrific scenes had become the norm. Many of my fellow Mojahedin supporters and members had been attacked, resulting in serious injuries and even death. There were media reports and pictures of supporters' eyes being gouged from their sockets. Thousands were arrested and imprisoned in response to rallies, meetings and leaders' speeches. To protest these cruelties, the Mojahedin leaders had decided to hold a demonstration on this day. They called on the Iranian people to join in and show their objections to Khomeini and his supporters. The demonstration was not announced publicly. Rather, supporters were encouraged to tell people whom they trusted and those they knew were unhappy with the regime to join the event.

In preparation, I had written a will that included the statement, I have accepted and chosen the Mojahedin ideology with awareness and understanding. And I will have no regret if I am killed in this challenge against Hezbollah. I hid the will at home amongst my books. After a shower and breakfast I left home around 6.30 am. I didn't tell any of my family members about the demonstration. Although they were aware that I was involved with Mojahedin, they were unaware of the extent of my activities. Still, from time to time they would ask me to quit my political involvement.

That day, I was wearing a long summer coat and veil (chador) in case I needed to carry any hidden items like pamphlets or newspapers. I went to a designated house in the suburb of Salsabil, the address of which I had been given by my supervisor. There were about fifteen people in the house. We had to be cautious and not enter the house all at once, so as not to alert the Hezbollah and government security forces. If they became suspicious, they would attack the house and destroy all documents, newspapers and tapes. We had a meeting before leaving the house, and were told by the leadership to defend against any Hezbollah attack, using any available weapons, such as a chain, syringe, stick, or knife. Up until then, we had endured two years of injustice, oppression and acts of cruelty by the government. Every day the pressure on the opposition had become tighter and more tense. I chose a chain and hid it inside my clothes. It was time to act.

We left the house around 10.30 am in groups of two or three. I left the house without a veil, making it easier to move around, especially as I didn't have to carry anything. I was wearing a thin summer jacket to my knees, with a pair of trousers and a scarf. I had two supporters under my authority. The demonstration was going to start from a few central points in Tehran, including Enghlab Square, Ferdosi Square, and Khyaban Pahlavi. Our group was supposed to gather in Enghlab Square. These central points were chosen, I believe, as they were always crowded with commuters and were main trading centres, so it was less likely that the government security and Hezbollah would be suspicious of the gathering crowd and attack the supporters before the demonstration started. The locations would also attract more people.

We caught a crowded bus to Enghelab Square. As always, the traffic was bad. We arrived there around 11.30 am. It was not wise to stop in one place, so we walked in the streets in pairs or alone around the Square waiting for the order to start the demonstration. I was with my supervisor, Maryam. Everywhere we walked we saw other supporters. We did not know them, but could recognize them as distinct from ordinary people or Hezbollah. The male and female supporters' dress code, the moustaches the male supporters grew, each female in a chador, the familiar hair styles, the slightly anxious look in their eyes and the simultaneous feelings of tension, solicitude and camaraderie were uniformly felt as we passed by. I even saw my University friend, Ali, who had initially encouraged me to start my political activities with Mojahedin. He smiled at us and passed by. The weather had warmed up – it was going to be a hot day. Seeing the other supporters gave me courage and lifted my spirits.

Finally, the order came and in less than a few minutes, Enghelab Square filled with the Mojahedin members and supporters. The demonstration started about noon and within an hour attracted a massive crowd. It was less than two years since the revolution and the people of Iran were unhappy, distressed and angry. Everywhere you looked was an ocean of people – estimates placed the numbers at around 500,000 persons. We started yelling slogans, demanding our freedom. As the crowd moved towards Ferdosi Square, there was excitement, anger, resentment and rage in the air. People had endured enough of lies, betrayal and suffocation.

The security forces had not expected such huge numbers, but with a growing awareness of the public groundswell, they acted swiftly, attacking protesters with knives, guns, sticks and other weapons. I witnessed a number of my friends being shot, some of whom were wounded and others were killed. Despite the show of force and violence, the protest continued.

We reached Ferdosi Square. The security forces and Hezbollah attacks became more intense and severe, even using machine guns and other heavy weapons. We started running. But the crowd was very thick and it was not possible to escape. People were screaming and trying to run away. The security forces drove at speed into the crowd on the Ferdosi overpass, sending bodies flying in the air. A few supporters were grabbed and thrown from the overpass to the ground. Anger was growing, so that when a section of the crowd found a lone Hezbollah member they surrounded him and beat him mercilessly. Some supporters used their weapons in defence, as they'd been instructed. It looked like a war zone.

Towards sunset, the protestors began to scatter. We were trying to escape the horrific violence. Some protestors tried to hide in people's houses. But the Hezbollah forces searched every house in the surrounding area and captured them. Everywhere we went, the security forces appeared. We were lost and trapped, not knowing whether to go right or left, to go straight or to turn around. A group of about 20 security forces surrounded our small group of half a dozen people. They seemed like wild animals rather than Muslim brothers, pulling our scarves, touching our breasts and cursing us with foul words. It was sickening. I felt powerless and wished for my life to end. We were pushed into a van.

In the van they blindfolded us before driving off for about 30 minutes. On the way, I thought they were taking us somewhere far from the city to drop us and let us go. This had happened in the past to supporters, but not to members. The van stopped. Our tormentors told us to get out and took us inside a building. Later my friends told me that we were taken to Komeite Enghelab Markazi (Central Islamic Revolution Committee), the Islamic government security forces' centre. These forces act separately from Army and Police. Still I had the chain with me. I knew I had to get rid of it, or I would be in huge trouble. I asked one of the guards to allow me to use the toilet. Luckily they did not object, and I was led to the toilet. I quickly hid the chain behind a rubbish bin, and immediately felt more relaxed.

My friends and I were then questioned and asked for our names and addresses. I gave them my name, but refused to give my address as I had many incriminating documents at home.

Given my refusal, I was placed in the van and sent to Evin Prison. I was not the only one, as most other supporters did the same, in line with Mojahedin policy. But the majority of the ordinary people who had just joined the protest on the street surrendered themselves and gave all requested details. A few followed us to the end.

My friends and I were physically, emotionally and mentally tortured and assaulted. They executed many of the prisoners, especially those they found carrying a knife or a chain or a syringe to defend themselves. That first night, while blind-folded, they took me and some other prisoners into a room and made us stand facing the wall with covered eyes till morning. Kicking and punching started immediately. One of the prison guards would kick our legs, lower back and other part of our body. He would also punch us to the head, with each punch so heavy that I thought I might lose my eye-sight. The blows to my lower back were so severe that I began my period out of its normal cycle. This torture continued until morning. If anyone cried from pain, they hit harder.

In the morning I was taken to a different room. I couldn't see and I didn't know who else was there. From another room I could hear a man crying and begging them to stop. They were torturing him. I could hear the punching and kicking. I couldn't stand hearing him crying. I wished I was in his place. The mental torture was worse than being physically tormented. I was kept in that room for a few hours and then transferred to an apartment in Evin prison. It was a multi-storey building that had probably been used previously as an office or a place for prison guards. All the windows were painted over so that prisoners could not see anything outside. This was to be my home for the next six months.

And so ended the first day of my five years, one month and five days of pain and suffering.

CHAPTER 2

Background on Iran

How did my life ever lead to such terrible experiences? What had happened in Iran in general and to me in particular that led to thousands of young people like myself being routinely taken into custody, tortured and even killed by their own government? To answer these questions, I need to provide my perspective on Iran's recent history and the story of my early family life.

The time from childhood to my teenage years is not comparable to my life after the revolution. I grew up in a family that allowed me and my siblings to experience freedom. I enjoyed my childhood and teenage life to a great extent, and will expand on this later in this chapter.

In Iran in the 1960s and 1970s, the majority of people had a variety of social activities available to them. After the revolution, people were deprived of these social freedoms. To understand what happened in my country, you need to know about Iran's geography, culture, and social outlook when the Shah was in power. I want to convince you that Iranians are not fanatically Islamic. To the contrary, Iranians are very friendly, hospitable and sociable people.

Iran is a beautiful country, located in southwest Asia and bordered by the Gulf of Oman (south), the Persian Gulf (south west) and the Caspian Sea (north). Iran's neighbours are Turkmenistan in the northeast, Azerbaijan and Armenia in the northwest, Afghanistan in the east, Pakistan in the southeast, Turkey in the northwest, Iraq in the west and Kuwait in the southwest. Azerbaijan and Armenia partially fall in Iran and the other part is in Russia. (Azerbaijan and Armenia were both under Iran territory, until they were occupied by Russia during the 19th century). Tehran, the capital of Iran, has a population of 84 million, with other major cities being Tabriz, Esfahan, Shiraz and Mashhad.

Iran used to be favourably compared to Paris by its neighbouring countries. When the Shah was ruling, it was heaven for Europeans and Americans, who could live in pleasure and enjoy social freedom. The country was modernized, though some minorities (people predominantly living in small villages) were still deprived of basic facilities such as water, electricity and gas. The government did introduce some reforms in 1962, with the aim of increasing literacy and education in the deprived areas. Overall, the country was progressing rapidly, soon to be brought to a halt with the 1979 revolution. Additionally, the majority of people were living at a reasonable standard and few people wanted to emigrate to America or Europe. If the people of Iran had also enjoyed political freedom, Khomeini and his supporters would not have gained victory. Lack of political freedom and the negative viewpoint of the world media influenced people to consider the Shah as a dictator, despite Iran becoming one of the most progressive countries in the world. My view is that if the Shah's power had been the same as the monarchy in England, we would never have ended up with the fanatics imposing their warped desires against our (Iranians) will. Back then we had only a few hundred political prisoners, but since the revolution this number has increased to tens of thousands.

The country's currency was very strong and the economy was stable. $1US was exchanged for 70IRR (Iranian Rial). In 2012, $1US was equivalent to 28,000IRR. Iran was also a powerful country in southwestern Asia and the rest of the world.

To provide an overall summary of the Shah's rule, the following summary of the Pahlavi Dynasty is provided by the Iran Chamber Society, which is a non-partisan and non-profit organization with the aim to promote Iranian culture and history. I have some misgivings about some of its particular perspective on Iran's history, which I will detail in what follows:

> The **Pahlavi dynasty** was the last Iranian royal dynasty, ruling for almost 54 years between 1925 and 1979. The dynasty was founded by a non-aristocratic Mazanderani soldier in modern times, who took on the name of the Pahlavi language spoken in the pre-Islamic Sasanian Empire in order to strengthen his nationalist credentials.
>
> The dynasty replaced the Qajar dynasty in the early 1920s, beginning on 14 January 1921 when 41-year-old soldier Reza Khan was promoted by British General Edmund Ironside to lead the British-run Persian Cossack Brigade. About a month later, under British direction, Reza Khan's 3,000-4,000 strong detachment of the Cossack Brigade reached Tehran in what became known as the 1921 Persian coup d'état. The rest of the country was taken by 1923, and by October 1925 the Majlis agreed to depose and

formally exile Ahmad Shah Qajar. The Majlis declared Reza Pahlavi as the new Shah of Iran on 12 December 1925, pursuant to the Persian Constitution of 1906. Initially, Pahlavi had planned to declare the country a republic, as his contemporary Atatürk had done in Turkey, but abandoned the idea in the face of British and clerical opposition.

The dynasty ruled Iran for 28 years as a form of constitutional monarchy from 1925 until 1953 and following the overthrow of the democratically elected prime minister, for a further 26 years as a more autocratic monarchy until the dynasty was itself overthrown in 1979.[1]

Mohammad Reza Pahlavi was the last *Shah* (King) of the Imperial State of Iran from 16 September 1941 until his overthrow in the Iranian Revolution on 11 February 1979. Due to his status as the last Shah of Iran, he is often known as simply **the Shah**.

Mohammad Reza came to power during World War II after an Anglo-Soviet invasion forced the abdication of his father, Reza Shah Pahlavi. During Mohammad Reza's reign, the British owned oil industry was briefly nationalized by Iranian Prime Minister Mohammad Mosaddegh until an Army coup d'état supported by the UK and the US deposed Mosaddegh, reinstalled the Shah, and brought back foreign oil firms under the Consortium Agreement of 1954.

Mohammad Reza introduced the White Revolution, a series of economic, social and political reforms with the proclaimed intention of transforming Iran into a global power and

---

1 - https://en.wikipedia.org/wiki/Reza_Shah

modernizing the nation by nationalizing key industries and granting women suffrage. During his 38-year rule, Iran spent billions on industry, education, health, and armed forces and enjoyed economic growth rates exceeding the United States, England, and France. The national income also rose 423 times over. By 1977, Iran's armed services spending had made it the world's fifth strongest military.

Mohammad Reza lost support from the Shi'a clergy of Iran and the working class due to alleged corruption related to himself and the royal family, suppression of political dissent via Iran's intelligence agency, SAVAK (including the arrest of up to 3,200 political prisoners), widespread torture and imprisonment of political dissidents, banishment of the Tudeh Party, U.S. and UK support for his regime, his modernization policies, *laïcité* or secularism, conflict with wealthy merchants known as bazaaris, relations with Israel, and clashes with leftists and Islamists.

By 1978, this political unrest became a popular revolution leading to the monarchy's overthrow. The Jaleh Square massacre, where his military killed and wounded dozens of protestors, the Cinema Rex fire, an arson attack largely but erroneously blamed on SAVAK in Abadan, defections and mutinies in the armed forces, the Muharram protests of over 5 million Iranians, and a meeting of western leaders that the Shah felt was a withdrawal of their support, made his position in Iran untenable. He left Iran for exile on 17 January 1979. While the Shah told his contemporaries in the West that he would rather leave than fire on his people, the number of protesters killed by his military is disputed, with the total number of people killed during the revolution ranging from 2,000 (Western figures) to 60,000 (figures of the Islamic Republic of Iran). Soon thereafter, the Iranian monarchy was formally abolished, and Iran was declared an Islamic republic led by Ruhollah Khomeini. The Shah died in exile in Egypt, whose president, Anwar Sadat, had granted him asylum.[2]

Khomeini and the rest of the Islamic leaders had claimed to bring the democracy into the country. Nevertheless they were just after power and to achieve this they committed the worst of crimes. This is still happening in my country.

Further, celebrating 2,500 years of Persian monarchy in 1971 was a positive and vital move in introducing Iran's rich ancient history, culture and religion to the world. Revolution was the consequence for the Iranian people who did not appreciate the Shah and his hard work.

It seems undeniable that the Iranian revolution was part of a worldwide political game between the 'superpowers'. Just when the country reached its highest achievements in terms of economic, social and political growth, the revolution took place.

The Shah's reign, like every other government, had weaknesses. But the country and people were well known and respected around the world. Worldwide attitudes and perceptions towards Iranians were completely different to now.

Today when I reveal my ethnic group I am often misjudged as a fanatic Islamic terrorist, not as a friendly, sensitive human being. The media must accept some responsibility for this. Generalisation of one individual's action is unfair and misleading. Fanatical Muslims represent a clear minority of the Iranian people. Why should I or the remaining majority be classed the same? We are as tormented as all free-thinking citizens by these dangerous and unthinking fanatics.

CHAPTER 3

My Family and Childhood

I was born on 23 September 1958, in a middle-class family in Tehran, Iran. I am the second eldest, with an older sister and three younger brothers. Even though my parents had their differences, I remember having a happy childhood.

In my family, we grew up freely in terms of what to believe or whom to support, though my parents always advised us not to get involved in politics.

My father had strict parents who did not let him to finish school. With secret help from his uncle he was able to graduate from high school. My dad studied for two years in the Iranian army's university and served two years as an Officer before leaving the army. He then studied for three years in a technical school, which belonged to the railway company owned by government, graduating and starting work as a superior train inspector. Later, he was transferred to the administration section and gradually promoted to managerial roles, finally becoming Product Releasing Manager in the Iran Railway Company until his retirement.

His first job as superior train inspector required him to constantly travel to different cities and this caused many arguments at home. My mother managed with three of us back then. She was also responsible for everything else at home; cooking, cleaning, bathing us and so on. My dad also helped her during the night with changing nappies and bottle feeding us, but this was not enough.

He had a background in politics. My father and his elder brother supported a political group called Tudeh. This group supported communist ideology. During World War II, Russian soldiers, under the communist banner, attacked and killed the Political Opposition members and generally mistreated them. My father quit politics soon after finding that the group he was supporting was not as honest as he thought. There were inconsistencies between their actions and the beliefs they taught to their followers. This was the reason my father always advised his children not to get involved in politics.

My mum was a most beautiful woman, with the looks of a movie star. My dad fell in love with her beauty and was devoted to her until he died. She was, and still is, a loving, caring and thoughtful housewife who was born into a wealthy family in Tabriz, in the northwest of Iran. Her father and uncle were some of the first people in the area to own cars – few people had cars in Iran at that time. During World War II, the Russian army attacked Iran at Tabriz and they stole her uncle's car. He was devastated and, being the older brother, my grandfather gifted his own car to his younger brother, even though it was a source of income. My grandfather did not appreciate his wealth and wasted most of his money by being over-generous and giving it all to his younger brother and his family. He also entered a second marriage and did not spend time with my mum and her siblings when they needed him.

My mum was a hairdresser for a while, working from home. However, constant housework and taking care of children did not allow her to continue her hairdressing business.

My parents were both born in Tabriz. Tabriz is located in East Azerbaijan province in the northwest of Iran. It was the capital at the time of the Qajar dynasty and is still an influential city in Iran. Tabriz has a very cold winter while the summer is pleasant, making it a desirable holiday resort. Tabriz has many historical monuments which have suffered repeated shocking earthquakes and various invasions during frequent wars, causing extensive damage to the city. Tabriz's historic bazaar complex was named as a World Heritage Site in 2010. In addition, there is an excavation site and museum in the city centre with a history that dates back 2,500 years. Shahgoli is another of the tourist areas in Tabriz famous for its beautiful summer nights.

I have many beautiful memories from my childhood, including travelling to different cities and beaches every summer. Travelling and sleeping the night on the country train was the most exciting and adventurous thing for me. Due to my dad's job, free tickets for two first-class cabins for the whole family was part of the package. As soon as we entered the train and found our cabins, fighting over the best bed would begin. All of us wanted to sleep on the top level of the bunk beds. As a child, sleeping on the top level was exciting. Compared to my siblings I was very quiet and usually the last to get anything. But still I would join the fight. The country train usually departed at night, around 5 pm. The fights in earlier years were between my sister, who is the eldest, the eldest of my brothers and me. My other younger brothers were too little. After coming to an agreement, running around from one wagon to another, marching through the train's restaurant, finding new friends, jumping up and down on the beds continued till we felt hungry and tired. It was time for food. My mum usually prepared sandwiches such as chicken with salad, beef patty with salad or potato salad, and we had it for dinner. They are all appetizing, mouth-watering and Iranian favourites, especially the potato salad. It has many ingredients and is very time consuming to make.

In later years, my younger brothers also joined the fights. By then my sister and I were teenagers and gave to the younger ones the chance to enjoy the excitements and adventures of these trips. For my sister and I things were changed. We were more enthusiastic to find new friends and have a tea or a soft drink in the train restaurant and make fun of everything and anything. We sat there and when we saw a young handsome man, whispering to each other and admiring his looks. When our eyes encountered his, we looked down and laughed with shyness.

When I was four or five years old, traveling to Tabriz and staying there with our relatives was a regular thing every summer for three or four years of my childhood. My aunties lived there, and I had many cousins who were much older than us. They were married and their children were the same age as us. I was eager for these holidays.

Tabriz is famous for its poplar trees. In Persian we call it the 'Tabrizi' tree. I still think of the sounds of the poplar leaves hitting each other with the force of wind and producing beautiful melody. The sound caressed our ears at night and, like a music box, helped us to sleep. We slept outside in the garden and covered ourselves with a warm quilt in the chill of night.

Shahgoli is another beautiful sight in Tabriz and its nights in summer are unforgettable. Tabriz climate in summer is very dry and hot and its winter is very cold and snows most of the time. Snow in some places is metres thick. Due to the heat, we went to Shahgoli at night. I can still hear the frogs and crickets singing aloud. That was the only noise we could hear in the silence of the night. We ran around, chased each other, screamed and made loud noises. Our voices echoed in the air and that created a harmony.

I also recall Lake Rezaeieh which, after the revolution in the late 1970s, was renamed as Lake Urmia. It is the third biggest saltwater lake and the largest lake in the Middle East. The salt content in the water is double the amount that is found in the oceans. The majority of its population is Assyrian. It is well known for its water therapy and mud therapy healing effects, a remedy for rheumatic, dermatologic and gynaecological problems.

To get to Lake Rezaeieh (Urmia) we had to travel by Country train to Bandar-e-Sharafkhaneh, a port in Lake Urmia, and from there we boarded a ship. The ship took us to Urmia's centre in two to three hours. During this short trip, sea sickness always troubled me. Going with my father onto the deck and breathing in the fresh air was the best medicine. After settling in a hotel and resting a while, the fun part would start, going for swim in the lake.

In the lake, almost everyone had a cucumber in hand. As soon as the salty water penetrated our eyes, we broke the cucumber in half and rubbed it into our eyes to wash out the salt. Due to the high quantity of salt in the water there was no likelihood of people drowning; everyone was a good swimmer in this lake.

It was also fun rubbing the mud all over our bodies and lying under the sun. Afterwards, swimming in the lake washed the mud off. The mud was black and smelly, but it really healed any pain. Many tourists travelled to Rezaeieh to take advantage of this remedial black mud. You could see them everywhere on the beach, lying on the sands with black mud covering their bodies. Females with bikinis loosened their tops and covered themselves with mud.

And then it was time to apply the mud to my parents' bodies. Whilst they were lying on the sands my siblings and

I would cover them with black mud. My mother always said that it healed her joint pain, the result of her hard work at home.

Leaving the motel every morning after breakfast to go to the lake for a picnic and a swim became our regular activity during the period of our stay in Rezaeieh. At sunset we took a taxi back to the motel, where my mother cooked the most delicious chicken meal for dinner. The aroma was mouth-watering: I could smell the sourness of the lemon, freshness of tomato and the bitterness of the pepper while the food was boiling on the fire. I was counting the seconds and waiting for the food to turn up on the dinner table, with my stomach making noises. After dinner we talked about the day's activities and planned the next day. Finally it was bed time. We slept like babies. This was our routine for the whole week during our holiday.

As we grew older, we changed the location of our summer vacation to the north of Iran; Ramsar by the Caspian Sea, one of the most popular summer resorts. We would stay in a motel which belonged to the Company where my dad worked.

Going to the beach, playing with balls in the water and flirting with boys was the most fun and enjoyable part of the trip. By noon almost everyone left the water to go to their room for lunch. The motel's restaurant would start serving around 1 pm, and the food was delicious and appetizing.

In the afternoon there were many different activities. Some parents usually had a nap before meeting their friends for a chat. For the younger ones, some would go back to swim but many would entertain themselves with other activities. My siblings and I, along with our friends, played table soccer, billiards and at night watched family orientated movies at an Open Air Cinema. After our week at Ramsar it was time to say goodbye to our friends, with the hope that we would see them again next year. Sometimes we would swap our contact details.

On the way back from one of our trips to the north of Iran, I woke up early in the morning as usual and found the train was still. At first I thought the train was at a station in one of the cities on the way back to Tehran. I was heading to the W.C. when all of the sudden I saw that the carriage next to ours was missing and the train was standing on a bridge. I woke my parents and my dad went to investigate. We found out that the train had been stationary for hours in that same position, standing on Veresk Bridge in Mazandaran, which serves the Trans-Iranian Railway Network between Mazandaran and Tehran. I don't remember how many carriages were attached to ours, or it might be that ours was the second last one. Gradually people got up and milled around in the train's corridor. It was very interesting for me and the other kids: I didn't want this to end. The authorities were trying to retrieve the separated wagons and link them to the train again. Nobody was allowed to get off the train. Outside, the scenery looked beautiful, as the north of Iran is very green. The roads wrap around hills and are carved into the forest. From a distance, the countryside resembled the most beautiful green velvet.

Besides going on a trip every summer, we did many other fun things. We had an apartment in a suburb called Shahre Ziba, which means 'Beautiful City'. This suburb was small with a wonderful boulevard, a beautiful park, and a large roundabout. There was greenery everywhere. In summer we would get together with our friends every night and picnic on the grass. The elders sat and talked and the younger ones strolled along the boulevard while the girls flirted with boys. The men drank: some became drunk and acted amusingly. Others played backgammon, played cards, listened to music or danced. Women talked about their day's work, their kids and gossiped. We stayed out until late, eventually returning home for sleep.

We moved house many times. The first house we bought was in the east of Tehran in a middle-class suburb called Narmak.

The highlight of this time was that my mum became pregnant with my youngest brother. Meanwhile, I spent lots of time with my cousin, Leila. After selling that house we upgraded to another one in the same suburb. We were there when the Shah celebrated 2,500 years of Persian monarchy. My dad had sold our TV so that we would concentrate more on our studies. However, we knew that the celebration would be extravagant and my mum didn't want us to miss this remarkable piece of history. One day she left home and few hours later came back with a beautiful colour TV. We were so excited.

My mum did not like the east of Tehran, so we sold the house and rented in a suburb called Eisenhower in the west. Mum learnt to cut hair and worked as hairdresser from home, but the pressure of housework was too high and she quit her job.

After a year we moved to another house in a suburb just next to Shahre Ziba called Istgahe Shahin. We rented this house as well, living there until we bought a nearby apartment. We lived in Shahre Ziba quite a few years while I studied at Farahnaz Pahlavi High School. Even when we upgraded the house and moved when I was fifteen to Aryashahr, a 10-minute drive away, I would still catch the bus and go to school in Shahre Ziba.

When I started my tertiary studies, I met many other students, both boys and girls, who became my friends. I enjoyed my tertiary studies. With my friend we would go mountain climbing or to movies, parks, parties and so on. This didn't last long, as after a year the revolution started. Many of my uni friends left Iran for the United States to study there. I was willing to follow them, but my parents were not happy for me to go on my own, as I was only 20 years old at the time. They were worried that I won't be able to protect myself and suggested my sister accompany me. However, she was very attached to the family and didn't want to leave Iran. Their other concern was the financial side of living in an overseas country, being worried that I wouldn't be able to support myself. Even though they could partially support me and I was planning to work there as a nanny, I still couldn't convince them to allow me to go and join my friends there. So I stayed in Iran. Less than a year after the revolution, the fanatical Islamic government closed all the universities under the name of the cultural revolution.

CHAPTER 4

University and Political Involvement

My parents always supported and encouraged us to undertake tertiary education. It was my dream to study at university. Getting into tertiary studies in Iran was not easy. Education fever was nation-wide, and competition was high. Almost everyone wanted to attend university. Higher education became part of people's culture. As a consequence of the high demand, the existing universities could not accommodate the large number of applicants. After Year 12, I attended a course to prepare myself for the entry exam. It was a comprehensive course that covered all the necessary subjects. I needed to get high marks. Even though my ranking was above the average, I did not get an offer in the first round, but succeeded in the second round.

I received an offer from the Tehran Institute of Technology and started studying accounting, even though accountancy was not my first choice. My girlfriend, Bahere, and I applied at the Indian embassy in Tehran for a student visa to study in India. I was planning to study journalism, having been influenced by the Italian journalist Oriana Fallaci. I read her book about the Vietnam War and admired her work and bravery in going into the war zone. I dreamt of becoming a journalist. However, due to the onset of the Islamic revolution, many foreign embassies closed their doors or held applications pending. My dream slipped from reach.

In September 1977, despite my lack of interest, I started in first year at the Tehran Institute of Technology. I was planning to apply for a degree course in the coming year. I met many students who became my friends, leading me to change my mind about changing my course. It was a new and enjoyable experience for me, especially as my high school had been girls only, and here I was mixing with boys and girls. After the Cultural Revolution, between 1980 to 1983, our university became a centre for the education of women, which upset many people from different levels.

Most of my weekends were spent with my friends from uni. We went climbing, watched movies, strolled in parks and gathered in each other's homes. We played cards, had dinner or lunch, and laughed a lot. At uni we played basketball, volleyball and table tennis. We sat in the cafeteria and chatted about movies, sports, food, our future, our studies and so on. Some of us felt love and affection for each other. I liked Ali. He was tall, dark and handsome. He was from Isfahan and had a sweet accent. I think he liked me too, as one day he gave me a pen with two hearts on it. That was a Parker metallic silver pen with one red and one blue heart. After the revolution he left Iran and I did not see him again.

Isfahan is in central Iran, south of Tehran, and is the third biggest city in Iran. It is full of ancient history and culture, and is a must-see place for tourists, known for its beautiful historical architecture, handcrafts, sweets and the hospitality of its people.

On 16 of January 1979, Shah fled Iran for Egypt. Over the previous few months there had been violent clashes between security forces and anti-Shah demonstrators. The exiled Ayatollah Khomeini entered Iran on 15 February 1979 and the people's uprising began.

I was about to finish the first year of my uni when the Islamic revolution took place. Khomeini promised the Iranian people many things, including democracy, freedom and autonomy. He promised freedom of speech and political activities. He promised to keep religion separate from politics. He promised free petrol, energy and even a share of income from the natural resources. Iran is a rich country with a variety of natural resources such as petroleum, gas, coal, chromium, copper, iron ore, lead, manganese, zinc, sulphur and more. We believed him. Contrary to his promises, he took everything away from us, including social and political freedom. It became compulsory for women to cover their head. Up until then, life was better – we had lived in a free society, and were not forced to hide our beauty behind a chador (hijab).

After the revolution, any opposition group that expressed their opinion or made statements against the regime was declared illegal.

My current political belief is to respect all people who are liberated and fight for freedom. Even though I believe in God, I do not believe in any kind of organised religion. I respect some creeds more than others. Humanity is more important to me than anything else. I believe in world unity and reject all kind of racial, ethnic, religious, gender and cultural inequality and discrimination.

The Iranian Cultural Revolution, along with political and social constraints and pressures, triggered the urge in me to form my political views and start my political activities. During 1980 to 1983 the fanatic Islamic government closed all universities in the name of the Cultural Revolution with the thought of purging all Western and non-Islamic influences from Iranian academia.

Up until then I was not involved in any kind of political activity. Although I was familiar with some of the ideologies, and attended rallies run by various opposition groups, I did not support any specific group. I found the left-wing groups weak and uncertain in their ideology. They seemed to float from one principle to another. The Mojahedin presented themselves to the people as being sincere and truthful. Their unprecedented Islamic beliefs made them very popular, forming the biggest opposition group.

In addition, my friend Ali, who I had met at uni, was the first within my group of friends to become involved with Mojahedin Khalgh. He introduced me to their ideology. I studied their books, attended their meetings, listened to their leader's speeches, and acquainted myself with their thoughts, ideas, strategies and goals. I joined a group of three supporters and started a discussion group, part of an organised program aiming to influence my friends and I to become Mojahedin supporters. I admired them for their humanitarian beliefs. That was how I started my political activities with Mojahedine Khalgh.

My involvement began with attending leadership meetings and speeches, distributing Mojahedin pamphlets, holding book stalls called Dake and joining ideological study groups. When we held book stalls, people would come and have ideological discussions with us. They were unhappy with the government's political system and were trying to find out if any of the opposition groups could save them and the country from its corrupted system. Hezbollah supporters tried to destroy our stall, unhappy that Mojahedin were gathering large numbers of supporters. Every day they attacked us, tore down our books, newspapers and pamphlets, and destroyed our settings. They hit us, swore at us and used abusive language. One day, as I was holding a bunch of Mojahedin papers trying to sell them, a man (intruder) suddenly appeared from behind to snatch my papers. I started running so fast that I could not believe I had that much energy in me. It was a hot summer day and I was fasting. People behind the wheels of their cars in the street stopped and started supporting me. They shouted encouraging words, inspiring my courage and bravery. At the same time, they were swearing at the intruder. After running for about 400 metres the man reached me and pulled the papers out of my hands and tore them into pieces. I was furious and shivering, thinking these people have no logic. Their logic is force, killing, torturing, deceiving, stealing and suffocating people's ideology and freedom.

Six months after starting my political activity, I was asked to wear a head scarf. Although this was against my beliefs, I had to compromise to follow my political views. I reasoned that the Mojahedin wore head scarfs to stop Hezbollah attacks on them and to protect themselves from being called nonbelievers, Marxists and hypocrites.

I wore a head scarf for ten years. I even wore a chador in some circumstances when I needed to disguise myself and/ or hide Mojahedin flyers, newspapers etc. When we had a meeting in one of the safe houses we wore chador in order not to be followed by Hezbollah and keep the house safe. Mojahedin supporters were easily recognised by their dress codes and styles. Wearing chador gave us the flexibility to carry newspapers and flyers with less apprehension.

Upon release from prison, I still wore a head scarf. It had become a habit. My shy personality at the time did not allow my instinct to prevail sooner. Back then head covering for women in public had become compulsory. The day that I fled Iran, I unveiled and to this date have never worn a head scarf again.

CHAPTER 5

Evin Prison

Following my first day of incarceration, I found myself in one of three rooms housing about 60 people. For the first couple of weeks we had no hot food. Our meals consisted of cheese, butter, jam, dates and bread. On 7 Tir 1360 (27 June 1981), they gave us our first hot food. We were so happy that we yelled with excitement. Using the excuse that we were making too much noise, the guards came in with sticks and took the food away from us. Whoever objected received a beating. The quantity of the food was never enough to feed everyone. We were hungry all the time. Later we discovered the reason for their brutal action on that day, Beheshti, so-called Chief Justice, along with many leading officials of the Islamic republic, were killed in a bomb explosion. Every time that something similar happened outside, revenge would be taken on the prisoners.

During these six months we were kept in ignorance of external events, with no access to any media reports or newspapers. The only way we could find out what was happening was when one of us was taken for interrogation and that person met a new arrestee. Although the prisoners were blindfolded, some would take the risk and exchange news.

We were on the second floor, with the first floor kept for male prisoners. Near the exit door, there was a hole that had been drilled for a telephone connection. The hole had a lead cover and, once removed, there was a channel to the first floor. We communicated with the men through this channel. Initially using a long rope, we would write our messages or any news we heard about outside and attach it to the rope and pass it down to the male prisoners. They would do the same for us. We had a daily set time to communicate, early in the morning before the prison guards started work. We would sometimes talk to them through this channel by putting our mouth to the hole while they put an ear to the other end, and vice versa. This way we were able to exchange the news that helped sustain us.

We did not have access to hot water for washing. Laundry powder was the only form of soap we had to wash our hair. As Evin Prison is located in an area that is surrounded by mountains, it has the coldest water you can imagine. Despite this we had no choice except to wash with this water or suffer various forms of hair and skin disease.

After one month, they turned on the hot water for the building and informed us that our apartment would have one hour to use the hot water. Imagine, 60 people, one shower for all, and a one-hour time limit! Quickly we organised a plan and divided ourselves into groups of four. Each group had just four minutes to stay in the shower. This became impossible in practice, with each group staying longer than their allotted time. The one-hour time limit soon passed and, finally, it was our group's term. I had a feeling that something bad was about to happen. Whilst we were in the shower, joking and laughing, two female prison guards suddenly came in with their sticks and forced us to leave the shower before we had finished. We put on our clothes and they took us out into the corridor.

Lajevardi, the head of Evin Prison, was informed. He was the cruellest, most heartless and vicious person I ever met. Executing prisoners for no reason came very easily to him. Even before Lajevardi arrived, we were made to stand on one leg and put a hand on our head for hours. If any of us fell down, then the prison guards made us stand again. We soon tired and our legs ached. When Lajevardi arrived, he took our names and shouted at us that we were disobedient prisoners for exceeding the one-hour time limit. What's more, he threatened that if he came across our names one more time he would sign our execution orders.

Whilst we were outside in the corridor, we saw many prisoners, all blindfolded, being taken to other apartments on the third or fourth floors. One of the prison guards made a surprising comment at that time: We know soon you will defeat the government and the Hezbollah and we will be your prisoners. We did not know why she should tell us this. As news came to us later, the unrest was reaching its peak at the armed struggle stage. Everyone was saying that soon the government would be conquered by the revolutionaries. The number of arrestees went up and everyday a number of prisoners were executed. The authorities had no shame and no fear of announcing the names of executed prisoners in the media.

Soon after, I was called in for questioning. Meanwhile, as I later discovered, my family thought I had been either killed in the protest or executed. They were searching for me among the dead bodies, from hospitals to prisons and monuments. Finally, they found my name on a prisoners' list and my father put in a request to visit me. In this way, the authorities found out that some of the details I had given were false. As mentioned, when first arrested, I did not give them all my correct details. I had many books and newspapers from Mojahedin Khalgh in my room at home. I knew that if they went there and found such incriminating evidence, they would most probably execute me and give my parents and the rest of my family a very hard time. They might also arrest them. So I gave them false information about my father's name and my home address.

I was taken blindfolded to the questioning room, which was in fact also the court, where my eyes were uncovered. The judge was Mohammad Gilani, the head of the so-called Islamic Revolutionary Court. A brutal man, he had ordered the execution of his two sons who were the members of Mojahedin. There was another mullah in the room.

Gilani asked me why I gave false information and I responded that as my dad was an elderly man, I did not want anyone to go my home. I told them that I was concerned he might have a heart attack. He then asked me what was I doing out on 30 Khordad. I said I had gone shopping with my girlfriend and we had become caught up in the demonstration. When he asked for my friend's name and address, I refused to give any more information. Gilani became very agitated, punching my head and threatening to execute me.

The whole exchange in the court took only few minutes. I did not have right of appeal nor to defend myself. A prison guard blindfolded me again and took me out of the courtroom. As I sat in the corridor, I thought they were going to take me for execution. I was praying and asking God to forgive me if I had made any mistakes in my life. But I still felt strongly committed to the ideology and the path I had chosen.

After about an hour a man approached with a stick in his hand. He told me to grab the other end of the stick – I was blindfolded. He took me to a room and said that I was sentenced to 75 lashes for giving false information. It was Ramadan and I was fasting. He asked me to lie on my stomach on the bare cement floor, then started hitting me with a long hose, from my shoulders down to my legs. The pain was unbearable. Each time he hit my lower back, I thought my body would split in two. I do not know how long it took, but when it finished I could not get up and collapsed. I was left on the floor of the corridor for about half an hour. Surprisingly, the man said he was sorry. I felt a measure of pity for him.

He took me to the prison's hospital, where I was given a cream to apply to my bruises. I did not know how bad my back was. When they returned me to the apartment, my friends came forward and helped me lie down. They checked my back and it was shockingly bruised, completely black. For couple of weeks I could sleep only on my front. My friends applied the cream to my back two or three times a day. The cream was helpful and the bruises disappeared quite quickly.

Though my treatment at this time was brutal, others fared even worse. One day they called another prisoner, Arasteh, for questioning. She did not have a strong political background and we therefore thought they would bring her back quickly. But night came and she did not return. Everyone was worried as we went to bed. At around 2.30 am we heard the door unlock and the prison guard led her in. She was stunned, not talking and staring at a corner. Her feet were swollen and bruised from a beating. We learned that she was also raped.

We had heard that before they executed a prisoner, if the prisoner was not married and was a virgin, she would be raped. But I could not understand why this happened in her case. She was no danger to this evil regime. Why would they want to execute her?

She had a very happy and mischievous personality, and would make us laugh. She made jokes and distracted us from the situation we were in, showing little interest in outside news. Overall, she was cautious and vigilant.

Later she told us how they sexually assaulted and raped her. There were two of them. One of the interrogators held her and the other raped her, and then they swapped. I struggle to even think about this vicious, heartless attack. We came to expect anything from these evil people, and considered them as spirit devils (Satanic). Arasteh's shocking treatment could be anyone's fate while in captivity. It took a long time for her to gain some of her natural spirits back. Later I asked her to describe the two men who raped her and to give me their names. I passed the information to a friend who was superior to me in the Mojahedin. She then passed the information to outside supporters in the hope that they could avenge her. I do not know of the outcome.

During the first six months, I witnessed much viciousness, brutality, violence and rape. It was all very heartbreaking. From the corner of a window, where the paint was missing, I saw the prison guards in front of the prison's main office, with their boots on, jumping up and down on a handcuffed prisoner lying on the bare asphalt ground. I could hear him screaming and crying from pain. The guards were laughing heartlessly and making jokes.

I saw prisoners in groups of eight or more, all with blindfolds and handcuffs, being taken for execution. They were in a line, with each prisoner holding the clothes of the person in front. A prison guard led the execution line holding one end of a stick, with the first prisoner holding the other end. Their feet were wrapped in white gauze and they could hardly walk. They were pulling their legs because of the pain, as their torture had included slashes to their feet. After they disappeared from our sight, about ten to fifteen minutes later, we would hear the gunshots.

This was my life in prison, and this is how it continued. But as I later found out, it very nearly didn't continue – not through my early demise, but quite the opposite. When later transferred to the main part of Evin prison, I met a young woman with an almost identical name to mine (her surname had an 'i' where mine had an 'a'). She didn't look like me, being smaller and thinner, with pale complexion and light brown hair. Like me, she was a Mojahedin supporter.

As she explained it, they had been going to release me. However, due to an administrative mix-up, they went to her ward instead of mine. As they started cross-checking her details, they found that her father's name didn't correspond with the information they possessed, and they realised that they had the wrong person. She was returned to her ward. Nothing happens quickly in prison, and no immediate action was taken. Outside, the situation became worse, and my release was forgotten amid the confusion. I was thus, by the merest chance of mistaken identity, to spend over five more years of physical and emotional torture and cruelty in prison.

How do I live with this? I believe it was my destiny, and I don't regret the five years. It made me a better person in terms of caring about others. In the past I felt for people's pain. Today I feel for others and take steps to help in any way within my power. It made me tougher towards difficulties, to be more patient and to appreciate life better. I am grateful that I am still alive and have the chance to experience and enjoy my existence. Although it destroyed my confidence, along with other psychological impacts, I have worked to overcome these setbacks.

CHAPTER 6

The New Evin Cell

After two months they transferred us from the apartment to the cells in the main part of Evin Prison. It was hard to know where we were going, as they blindfolded us for the walk to our new cells. I watched from under the eye cover, trying to remember the path, imagining that maybe one day I might have a chance to escape. But it was impossible to remember the surroundings, as I could see only my feet. Besides, security around Evin Prison was very tight and escape was impossible.

After about 15 minutes we arrived at the destination, Ward 246, second level of Evin Prison, and we were crammed into a single cell. Each cell was about four by six metres, and held about 50 to 60 prisoners. For the first week or so the cell's door was locked. We could go to W.C. three times a day: morning, noon and night. If someone had a kidney problem, she had to call the guards many times until they would open the door and let her to use the toilet. They allowed one prisoner at a time out of the cell for refreshment, then moved on to the next

41

cell. To keep us on edge, they made everything complicated, enigmatic and ambiguous, though it is possible that they were scared for their own safety.

We did not know who was in the other cells, as the cell walls were built from cement and each cell had a very heavy steel door, which had a little window. At the beginning it was difficult to sleep at night. We could sleep only by lying on one side. In the middle of night, if we needed to stretch our hands and legs, or change sides, we sat, stretched and then changed our sleeping position.

After a week they opened all the cell doors and we could see the other prisoners. I spied one of my friends who had been under my supervision before the arrest. I hugged her. She told me that she was arrested while distributing Mojahedin pamphlets. Her capture took place after the initial round of arrests on 30th Khordad 1360, which she'd been able to avoid. I was so happy to see her. As it was not long since she was arrested, we were able to talk about what was happening outside. This was the only way that we could get the outside news, from those prisoners who were recently arrested. Media reports were not accurate and, anyway, we did not have access to any media or newspapers. Suddenly, in the middle of our conversation, the prison loudspeaker announced a few names and asked them to collect all their belongings and be ready for the next announcement to leave that ward.

My friend was one of them. She looked pale and anxious, telling me that they were taking her for execution. I did not believe her and told her, surely not. I asked her why she thought she would be executed. What were her charges? She replied, distributing and carrying Mojahedin flyers. I told her they would probably transfer her to Ghezel Hesar prison for the rest of her sentence. I believed that in my heart! I couldn't imagine that anyone could be executed for something so insignificant.

Before they called them for the last time, we all gathered in one of the cells. We started singing children's songs to make them laugh. We kissed them goodbye. And, finally, we sang them the Mojahedin anthem. They were proud. They did not regret their actions. They had a fear of dying but nothing else.

I could still not believe they were taking my friend for execution. After half an hour, they called them for the final time and took them away. Thirty minutes later we heard the gun shots. From a distance, it sounded like the crash of layers of heavy tinfoil. It then became clear to me that she had been executed. I felt very sad and depressed and was in tears of grief and helplessness. It could happen to every one of us.

That was my first experience of such a profoundly depressing incident. Executions then became daily events. It inspired me to be stronger and more determined in my resistance. Why should anyone be deprived of their freedom, tortured, brainwashed and executed for their beliefs?

For our guards, there was no difference between young and old. They tortured and executed many elderly persons. I met an older woman whom we called Mother Zakeri. She was a brave, fearless elderly woman in her early seventies. She had four or five children who were all Mojahedin supporters except for one who was a fanatic Hezbollah. He held a high position in the Islamic government, and had his family, including his mother and sister, arrested and jailed. After I was transferred to another prison, I heard that Mother Zakeri had been executed. Another of her sons (Ebrahim) was a member of the Mojahedin and played an important role in the Mojahedin uprising. He was in a Mojahedin camp in Iraq at the time. Mother Zakeri's crime was that she was the mother of a Mojahedin member – she stood up for what she believed is right and did not repent. For this she was executed.

First photo from left – my cousin, myself, my father, my cousin, my sister standing between my father and my cousin

My Father when he was student in the Army university

My mother when she was carrying my sister her first child

I was 5 or 6 months old

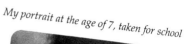

My portrait at the age of 7, taken for school

Myself when I was 5 years old

Primary school – I am the second person from left standing

My father, my mum, my auntie (Roghi) my late cousin's wife, my late cousin and in the front from left (myself, my brother Hossein, my sister Parvaneh)

My nieces, Maral, Ghazaleh from left and their friends

My father, my sister Parvaneh sitting on his lap, my mum, my cousin (Tayebeh), her late husband (agha Mehdi), My older cousin's late husband (aghaye Mirnezami), Pari (my extended cousin)

I am the one wearing glasses.

My mother, Parvin, newly married to my father and my cousin, Ozra

A portrait of me when
I was 16 or 17

A portrait of
myself, when I
was 17 years old

A photo of our
dance group when
I was a high school
student (I am the
second person from
left standing up) I
still have contact
with Venus, the 4th
person standing up
and the first person
from left sitting.

Our dance group
during an Iranian
traditional dance.
I am the one in the
middle from the right

My beautiful
mother. She looked
like a movie star.

My cousin (Shahram),
myself with big curly
hair, far back my mum
and my auntie (Masi)

A portrait of me when I just finished my last exam in year 12

My mother, myself (only one month after release from the jail. I was still wearing scarf), my sister, front row, my nieces (Maral and Ghazaleh and their friends)

Photos with my brother, Masoud and friends when we were in Turkey. I am the one sitting on the right

Photos with my brother, Masoud and friends when we were in Turkey. I am the one sitting on the right

Photo with our
house mates,
Amir from left
and Mammad in
the middle

Myself and my best
friend Bahereh dancing
in one of our girlfriend's
wedding. Here I was still
at High School.

One of prisoner's daughter who was
born in the prison and mother sent her
out in her parent's care

couple of months
after release
from the prison,
siting in our
little garden and
enjoying the
sunshine

2008 when I graduated in Australia – I graduated from Swinburne university – I completed the bachelor of business majored in Accounting and Finance

Bonney Leder Copyright 1998

Boxing day 2019, with Barbara, Tina, Roger and Antonette at my home (my tango class friends)

A photo from our front yard in Shahrak Cheshmeh

A photo with my parents when I was in Turkey waiting to come to Australia

I used to go to a nice coffee shop sit there and write. This was taken at Matto café in Heidelberg

Meeting up with David Murphy my editor to discuss about my book. This was taken on the 5th March 2020 at Laurent café in Camberwell

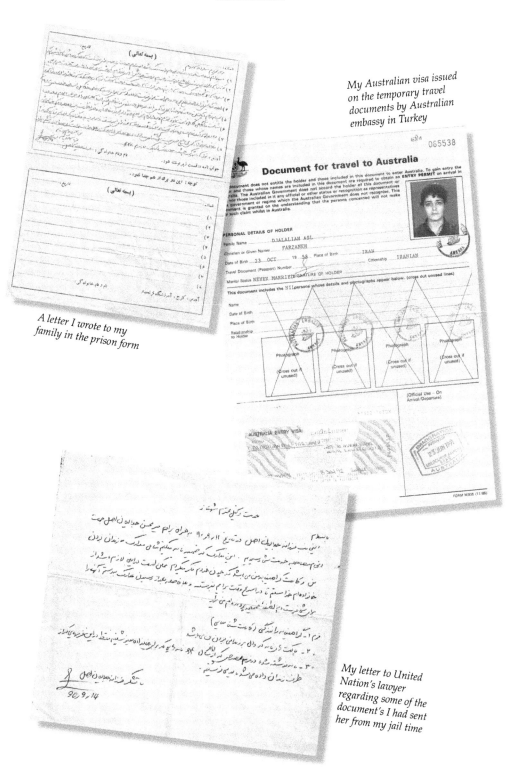

My Australian visa issued on the temporary travel documents by Australian embassy in Turkey

A letter I wrote to my family in the prison form

My letter to United Nation's lawyer regarding some of the document's I had sent her from my jail time

Confirmation of Australian visa issued and granted for me

Telegram arrived from UNHCR in Ankara for us to go there and fill in rrf form to receive some financial support. We were in Nevsehir at that time

```
42915 ank6 tr

nsehir30 tr*
42915 ank6 tr
6039 ankara telex 6019 35 7 12 1000 - 8 12 0139

jalalianasli farzaneh jalalianasli mir mohsen j-371 j-370
350 evler 1. sok no:31
nevsehir

ankara(unhcr)
pls come to unhcr on 10/12/1991 to fill rrf form and show the
letter at the gate

col 350 1 31
nnnn
```

Poem was about me written by my father's friend who was 25 years my senior. He proposed to me in Turkey

Envelope I sent letter in it from the Ghezelhesar prison

Envelope I sent letter in it from the Ghezelhesar prison

Letter I wrote to my family from Ghezelhesar prison

Letter I wrote to my family
from Ghezelhesar prison –
The painting was for my
niece, Ghazaleh that was
born when I was in prison

The envelop that my
father's handwriting
is on it, sending me
a letter

CHAPTER 7

Relocation to Ghezel Hesar

On 9 February 1982, after eight months of captivity in Evin Prison, I was transferred to Ghezel Hesar prison in Karaj, 20 kilometres north-west of Tehran. I was sentenced to ten years imprisonment. As it turned out, I spent four years and five months in Ghezel Hesar prison. The day before my transfer, on the 8 February, Hezbollah attacked the safe house where Mousa Khiabani, Ashraf Rabii, and seventeen more Mojahedin members were living, killing all of them. Ashraf Rabii was the wife of Masoud Rajavi, the Mojahedin's leader in exile. The couple had a son, Mostafa, aged 2 or 3, living with Ashraf, his mother at the time. Mousa Khiabani was the second person in ranking within Mojahedin, being the organisation's Commander in Iran.

The prison guards gave us the news, as we had no access to media. They were happy to unveil the ambush at the Mojahedin leader's safe house. I did not believe them when they told us the news, thinking that they said it to eradicate our trust, faith and confidence in our fight against corruption, destruction and cruelty that was growing day by day.

It was a cold winter day when they called my name, along with a group of other prisoners, over the loudspeaker. We were told to be ready with all our possessions in one hour. I collected all my belongings and said goodbye to all my friends. I was blindfolded again. I knew they were taking me to Ghezel Hesar to spend the rest of my sentence there.

We walked some distance for about seven minutes or so. They then directed us to get into a bus. After few minutes' drive, the bus stopped. They took us to a field that was frosted and slippery. The freezing cold penetrated my skin, so that I could feel it in my bones. The Prison guards were happy and laughing loudly. They removed the blindfolds and made us walk through the dead bodies of the 19 members of Mojahedin who had been ambushed the day before, as they lay on the icy floor. Lajevardi, the big Satan, was there, carrying Moustafa, Masoud Rajavi and Ashraf Rabii's son. The poor young boy was forced to see his mother's dead body frozen on the floor. Some of the prison guards were lifting the Mojahedin members' bodies by the head and dropping them on the floor, laughing louder. The skin of the bodies was pale, and the lips were blue. I felt dizzy, about to collapse. One of the female prison guards, who was walking next to me, noticed it. She held me and with a teasing tone asked me if I was disturbed that our leaders were being killed. I gathered myself and with pride said that I was fine. I didn't want to give her any pleasure by revealing my sorrow and disturbance. I don't remember how long they kept us there, perhaps five or ten minutes. We were then blindfolded again and got into the bus to be taken to Ghezel Hesar.

Ghezel Hesar is in Karaj province, about an hour's drive from Tehran. The prison is normally for criminals, but since the number of political prisoners exceeded their expectation, and was still increasing, after sentencing the prisoners in

Evin they transferred them to this jail to spend the rest of their prison term. To my memory, Ghezel Hesar had about 12 wards. The political prisoners were kept separate from the criminals.

We arrived there in the afternoon. The head of Ghezel Hesar was Haji Davoud Rahmani, a tall man with blue eyes, a beard and moustache. I have a point in describing him in detail that I would tell later. The first words he told us was that we will each be released from the jail as an old lady, wearing glasses, holding a walking stick, with dentures and so on. It would thus be better for us to obey the rules, otherwise we would suffer the consequences.

I was taken to Ward 4, which had about 16 cells, each cell containing 10 to 12 prisoners. In each cell there was a three-level single bed, with the middle level designated as a kitchen (more detail later). I was put into cell number 8, where there was not enough bedspace for all of us. Four of us slept in the two beds, two in each bed, with the rest on the floor. We had a schedule to rotate our sleeping spot. If one of us had a medical condition, that person would sleep in a fixed spot. The floor space next to the bed and bottom end of the bed was very narrow. Still two of us slept in those spots, which we called the grave.

The first prisoner that I met in Gheze Hessar was Tayebeh, who oversaw Ward 4. I initially thought she had repented and joined Hezbollah. Later, I found out that she still strongly believed in Mojahedin. This was her tactic to infiltrate the jail system. At our first eye contact, she blinked and smiled at me. She was trying to give me the message that she was still one of us. She was a very friendly, mischievous and active person.

CHAPTER 8

Life in Ghezel Hesar

Life in Ghezel Hesar was different. Everyone had already received their sentence and the pace was slow. Although we did not have any activities in Evin, we still had some connection to the outside world and what was happening out there. In Ghezel Hesar we were like dead people waiting for the guards to dictate to us our daily activities. We did not have our own schedule, as everything was programmed for us. First thing in the morning we were woken up before sunrise for prayer. Then it was time for cleaning and breakfast, with food delivered to us from the prison's kitchen. The kitchen was managed by male prisoners, though under strict supervision. The prison gave the kitchen the list of food that could be prepared daily. The amount of food for each ward was also stipulated by the prison.

We had TV, but again it was controlled by the prison's authority. Whether or not we could watch TV depended on the outside situation. Our favourite to watch was the children's program. Other than that, everything was censored or not worth watching. I remember a program called Mice City, the funniest kids' program ever. The characters I remember included Sarmaee (which means someone who always feels cold and shivers) and Kopol, who was a chubby and funny character. There was also Einaki, which refers to someone who wears glasses. He was the smartest and was always studying, what we now call a nerd. Mice City was on every weekday at 4 pm. At that time, everybody would run and sit in front of the TV to watch the program. It was the prison guard's favourite as well. I discovered this one day when I was sick and taken to the prison clinic. On my return I noticed one of the guards calling the rest of his friends, telling them that Mice City was starting.

Apart from this, everything was under their control. They would try to brain wash us with their religious programs that were broadcast 24 hours a day. We were forced to listen to their leaders, such as Motahery's Islamic moral speeches, Motahery being one of their ideological leaders.

Sometimes, depending on the outside situation, the guards would give us a newspaper. We were thirsty for any books or papers and reading materials. We read every word, even the advertisements. We even appreciated their books, that in most part were nonsense. Still, from within the content we were able to glean useful information. In addition, reading kept our brains engaged and helped to pass the time easier. We tried to take advantage of any little opportunity. For example, after reading the propaganda materials, we discussed, analysed and criticised the illogical and irrational points. We thus didn't allow our time to pass idly by.

We were not allowed to talk among ourselves about politics or news that we heard about the outside situation or unrest. Any group gathering that looked suspicious resulted in punishment, such as deprivation of TV and reading materials. In addition, suspect prisoners were sent to punishment wards. To counteract this, we formed an organised group with a leader named Maryam. We called her Mother Maryam. She was pregnant when she was arrested, and delivered her daughter in the prison's clinic. Her daughter was a year old when Maryam sent her out, giving custody to her parents. Her husband was a member of Mojahedin who had been executed. She was a young blonde woman with small frame, in her late 20s. She never took off her scarf in front of anyone. I thus never saw her without a scarf. After I was released from jail, I heard that she was also executed. However, last year, after more than 35 years, when I met two of my prison friends here in Australia, they explained that she had not been executed.

Ward 4, where I was imprisoned, had a yard where we walked every afternoon. The guards gave groups of us access to the yard at certain times of the day. For me that was every afternoon from 4 pm for couple of hours. We walked in pairs pretending that we were making normal conversation. We talked in low tones so that the others could not hear us, as there were some prisoners who had repented and were spying for the prison authority. I would liaise with Mother Maryam, passing information from other members to her. She would also pass new information to me. All these transfers of news happened in the yard whilst we were walking. Once I had passed everything to Mother Maryam, I would speed up walking and move some distance from her. Then another friend/member would join me in the walk. This process was repeated until everybody in the group received the latest news. The news would come from newly arriving prisoners who had been transferred to Ghezel Hesar or during family visits. Prisoners who were allowed contact visits had a better chance of receiving news from their parents.

One of the group members was Sima, who was also a blonde and a very soft-spoken young girl. About 18 or 19 years old, she was very kind and had a lovely personality. She was very eager to be part of the group and did not fear that the authority might find out that she was one of us. She had an older sister who later transferred from Evin Prison to our ward in Ghezel Hesar. Sima had told me that her sister was high in rank within Mojahedin supporters. She told me that her sister had also been arrested but was still in Evin. After she joined Sima at Ghezel Hesar, Sima discovered that her sister had repented and had changed her ideology from Mojahedin to Hezbollah. She was spying for the prison authority. Once she observed that Sima was in daily contact with me, she became suspicious that some sort of organised activity was happening. She reported me to the prison authority. As a consequence I was sent to the Punishment Ward, Ward 8, details of which I will explain later. I denied any wrong-doing. I was told to avoid going to the Punishment Ward, I must repent. I accepted to sign a letter of apology. It was an accepted Mojahedin tactic to pretend repentance to survive. But then they said that my repentance must be recorded and played on TV and media. I rejected that and as a consequence was transferred to Ward 8. I was kept in Ward 8 for a year or so. During the night of my transfer many astonishing things happened that I will describe in the next chapters.

CHAPTER 9

Transfer to Punishment Ward

As mentioned, my friend's sister reported me to the authorities and, as a result, I was taken to Punishment Ward 8. This happened one day before my next family visitation. It was my mum's turn to come, and it was the middle of winter. The windows in this ward were broken and the authorities ignored the consequences. We did not have enough warm clothes or blankets to warm ourselves up. When my mum came for her visit, she was so anguished and stressed that she could not even cry. Her thyroid had swollen and become so enlarged that I worried for her health. She had heard that the ward's windows were broken, and had brought me some warm clothes and a blanket, but the prison authorities would not let her bring them in. I tried unsuccessfully to calm her down by saying that the windows had been fixed.

After visitation time was over and we had finished our dinner, we were told that Haji Rahmani, the head of Ghezel

Hesar Prison, was coming to the ward. We were told to put on our chadors (hijab) and be ready. We felt panicked, though we were whispering and giggling. We knew he would only come when something bad was to happen. I whispered to my friend that I was worried what to do when he saw me. I knew he was going to pick on me just because I had green eyes and was wearing glasses. He was very sensitive towards prisoners with coloured eyes and anyone who wore glasses. I had both.

I decided to take off my glasses and keep my eyes down. He arrived to the ward and started one of his usual speeches. He told us how some of us had not obeyed the jail's rules and had been rebellious. How we were going to age in the prison or our dead bodies would be sent out. He then read out the names on his list and asked them to come out of the queue. These names had been reported to the prison authorities by our ward's prison guard. The prison guards checked on us daily and if they became suspicious, they reported it to the authorities. He then started marching along the rest of the queue. He picked a few prisoners at random, just by their looks. He then reached me. I was trying not to look at him. But, as my friends have observed, I have distinguishing features that everyone remembers. He called me out. He then said to all of us who he had chosen to be ready to be taken to another ward of the jail where the punishment was even more severe. I thought of my mum and how unwell she had been that day. I thought that if they take me somewhere harsher, she would not survive. I talked to the ward's prison guard, and told her about my mum and her poor health. I told her that I was new to the ward, and that I had not done anything wrong to be taken to the other punishment ward. She felt mercy towards me and spoke to Haji Rahmani. Amazingly, he changed his mind and asked only for the ones whose names were on his list to be taken to the other ward.

Conditions in the Punishment Ward were unbearable. Numbers of prisoners were forced into a small and narrow cabin-shaped room. The prisoners crammed inside could only sit facing their heads towards the wall, while listening to the prison's brain washing broadcasts all day. They were taken to use the toilet three times a day, and were denied any visitation. I heard that some of them had bruised and wounded buttocks due to long hours of sitting. Some of them could not bear the conditions and repented.

In Ward 8, where I was imprisoned, the living conditions were poor. Hygiene was minimal, and we had no access to a yard. The cell's windows were small and too high, so that the time that I spent there, I did not see any sunshine. We hung our washed clothes on the cell's bars. Many of us caught a skin disease called Gall, which comprised of raised sores on the skin, caused by rubbing or chafing.

It was a disastrous situation. I couldn't sleep at night. My body was itchy. It felt as though something was moving under my skin, especially around my knees. The prison doctor prescribed an ointment for us, and we had to boil all our clothes. I also caught head lice. My hair had by then grown long, and I had to cut it short to get rid of the lice. My friends helped me by picking off the eggs stuck to my hair one by one and squashing them to kill them.

In addition, as there was not enough food, we scavenged the old bread that was to be thrown away and ate it.

Everywhere in the jail were mice, especially in Ward 8. Sometimes they died in our beds. They would sneak into our beds and when we rolled over, some were squashed and died. The mice climbed everywhere and attacked our food. We hung some of the food such as pistachios and other nuts from a rope we attached in the cell from one side to the other.

In this ward, we did not have any reading materials. Time passed very slowly. As we were completely isolated from the other part of the jail, the only way we could hear any news was when one of us was sick and had to be taken to the clinic to see the jail doctor. It then depended on whether there was another prisoner from one of the other wards who could find a way to communicate.

I was kept in this ward for nearly one year. I was then transferred back to Ward 4. I do not exactly know why this happened. It may have been due to Ayatollah Montazeri putting pressure on the government to ease some of the overcrowding of prisoners. Or it could have been my parents' activity outside the jail to free me. After being back in Ward 4 for a day I was called to the office. There was a mullah sitting there. He asked me if I was happy to repent and for it to be recorded and shown in the media. He said if I did that, I could be freed from the jail. I said to him I had not done anything wrong that required repentance. He got angry and told me that I had not changed, and thus must stay in jail.

Ayatollah Montazeri was one of the leaders of Iran's 1979 revolution. In 1989, he fell out with other leaders over government policies, criticised the government and claimed it infringed on people's freedom and their denials of their rights. It was through his influence that some of the prisoners were released from the jail.

Emotional torture

Before I was transferred to Ward 8, they had started the emotional torture and pressures on the prisoners. For about two months we were woken up before sunrise, prayed and before breakfast were forced to sit on the floor of the jail's corridor to listen to the repentant video and/or their leaders' ideological speeches. At around 7 am we went inside the ward to have our breakfast. After cleaning the kitchen, we again sat in the corridor to listen to the same monotonous broadcasts. This was repeated at lunch time and dinner time, until it was time for us to sleep. This pattern continued in Ward 8.

Tea from shower water

In Ward 4 at Ghezel Hesar, they turned on the hot water daily at 11 am. At that time one of us waited in front of the ward's door and as soon as the prison guard knocked at the door to say that hot water was on, every cell's kitchen shift prisoner ran to the shower to fill a big tin bucket. This was how we made our daily tea. We found it funny and laughed about it. Just imagine 24 or so of our friends with tin buckets in their hands running to the bathroom at the end of the ward, across from the entrance door. The cells were around a big hallway, with twelve on one side and twelve on the other. As the kitchen's shift was doing this, some of the other prisoners ran to grab their things to go for their scheduled shower. Some of us watched TV, while others chatted.

Such activities brought excitement to the ward. Little things would engage us, bringing life and vivacity, keeping most of us brave and positive about life. We kept our souls in good spirits and never gave up life. However, we had fellow prisoners who were suffering from deep depression. They did not want to have contact with anyone, refusing to communicate. They sat quietly in the corner of their cell, hugging their knees and retreating to their own silent world. We didn't know what their thoughts were about life in prison. Some refused to see their family when they came to visit them, even though these families were coming from other cities.

In the jail we became very creative. With cartons and boxes, we made multilevel cabinets for our kitchen. As previously mentioned, we had designated the middle level of the three-level bed as the kitchen in each cell. The cabinets looked nice and clean. With self-adhesive patterned plastic, we covered the cartons and boxes that we had transformed into the cabinet's shelves. The plastic protected the shelves from oily food and dirt. After breakfast, lunch and dinner, the assigned labourers (kitchen shifts) for the day tidied up and cleaned everything.

We had a schedule for each day's kitchen chores, with two of us responsible for the work. The list was rotated so that we all took a turn. Much of our food was either bought from the Prison or brought by our families. Families could only bring canned food such as tuna and nuts. Home-made food was not allowed.

Stone Grating

The other creative hobby in the jail was a craft we called stone grating. We found the stones in the jail's yard. We checked them with a syringe's needle to see if they could be grated, as some stones were hard to scratch. With a stone foot file, we flattened the stone into different shapes, such as a heart, triangle or circle. We would then draw or write a manuscript (phrase or word) on the stone. Some of our friends were talented at drawing and hand-writing manuscript. Then we started grating with a needle from a syringe, the only sharp object we could obtain. We patiently scratched around the drawing or the phrase with the needle. Horses have always amazed me: I think of a horse as a very beautiful, powerful and proud creature. I found a black stone and asked a friend to draw a horse on it. I paid a lot of attention to scratching in the fine details and after finishing it, I was very proud of what I had achieved.

CHAPTER 10

Visitation

Visitation was possible only once a week, on Friday. Back then in Iran, just one day in the week, Friday, was designated as the weekend. Currently some work places have two days, Thursday and Friday, as the weekend.

Our house was in Sharhrak Cheshme, in the North-west of Tehran. From Sharak Cheshme to Ghezel Hesar Prison in Karaj it was about 48 kilometres. Due to the long distance, my parents were only able to visit every fortnight. They would take turns, with one fortnight my father visiting, and my mother visiting two weeks later. It was too hard for my parents to come every week, with their busy and stressful lives. My sister, Parvaneh, was married and had her first baby girl, Ghazaleh, during the first year I was in prison. Soon after, she was pregnant with her second daughter, Maral. My eldest brother, Hossein, was also married, and his wife was pregnant with their first child. My middle brother, Amir, was in his last years of high school and was planning to leave Iran. And my youngest brother, Masoud, had just started college where he was studying Electronics. My parents were closely involved with all these family responsibilities, making it hard for both of them to visit at the same time. In addition, my father had a real estate business and could not close the shop every Friday, as just like everywhere else in the world, many people allocate their weekends to look for real estate.

My mother used a taxi or public transport to come to Ghezel Hesar. When I think of all the suffering and difficulties they endured, I feel very sad and depressed. This was especially true in winter, when it snowed and roads were frosty and slippery. Though my father could drive to visit me, it took two hours to get from home to the prison, and my father had to equip his car tires with chains so that the car did not slip on the road.

My parents faced all these difficulties for visits which were very restricted. In the cabins where the visits took place, they were kept behind a glass window. We talked using a telephone intercom. On each side there was a seat and a telephone, with a desk attached to the window. The telephone intercom hung from the wall. The cabins were dull and ugly, separated by walls, with no doors.

Siblings were not allowed to visit. During the second year of my imprisonment, I had my first surprise visit. My mother was braver than my father. One Friday, when it was her time to visit, she brought along my sister and her baby daughter, Ghazaleh, just one year old. This was first time I had seen my oldest niece, as when I was arrested, my sister was pregnant with her. When she visited, she was pregnant with her second child, Maral. I was so happy and pleased to see my sister after two years in prison, and to see my niece for the first time. Everyone says Ghazaleh looks like me, and she is now a grown-up beautiful lady. Sometimes, when I look at her, I see myself and feel the resemblance. My sister was also happy to see me. We both cried. At first, I thought that she had entered with permission and so didn't ask her how she came in. But after a few minutes, the prison guard who was checking the cabins suddenly noticed that I had two visitors. She asked my sister her relationship to me, and as soon as she learned she was my sister, she terminated the visit and forced them to leave. I asked her to allow my mother to stay for the rest of the time, but she refused. Even though I was not happy with the shortness of the visit, at the same time I was very pleased to see my only sister after two years of separation. Before she was married, we were very close, doing many different things together, including shopping, parties, gathering with our friends, picnics and discos. After she married, there was a gap in my life and I tried to fill this gap with my friends and other activities.

The closure of the universities, my parent's lack of support for me to go to America to join my university friends, all added to my tendency to become politically active. As a young member of society, I could not accept the government's decision to close those sacred places, the universities. I call them sacred because I believe universities can and should be one of the places for human growth (mentally and emotionally). In societies where education is minimal and unemployment is high, young people find refuge with drugs, sex and worse.

My second surprise visit was after three years of imprisonment. That day my mother brought along my grandmother, Robabeh, and my oldest auntie, Batool. As I later learned, at first they were not allowed in. They cried and asked to be let in, pleading that they were afraid they would die soon and never see me again. Thankfully the prison guards let them in. My mum told the prison authorities that my auntie was my grandmother from my father's side. My auntie was 77 years old at the time of the visit. Out of respect, everyone called her Khanoom baji, which in Persian means lady sister. She was the eldest among my father's siblings, with my father being the youngest. There was a big gap between the two, as my father was only 59 back then. At the time my auntie married, women would marry as young as 14. That was why they believed my mother's story and allowed her in.

As soon as I saw her, my heart sank, as I felt it was the last time I would see her. We were all crying, tears of happiness and tears of separation at the same time. When they were leaving, I looked into my auntie's eyes and said goodbye! That was it. She died a few months later.

CHAPTER 11

Illness in Prison

All of us suffered from depression, some to lesser degree and some more severely. I also suffered from depression. The living conditions, the emotional torture, the abandonment, isolation and being far from the family were the main reasons. Our life was encapsulated in a prison ward and, if we were lucky, we could walk for an hour or so in the prison yard.

I didn't know that I was depressed until I was released from the prison. For a few weeks, I did not wish to see any relatives. My family, especially my mother, father and my sister, were all very supportive. They asked the relatives, who were wishing to come and see me, to wait until they let them know. I had lost a lot of weight, being only 42 kilos – my height is 160 cm.

Though I suffered from depression, my family suffered even more. I adjusted to the surrounding conditions in which I was living. Early in my incarceration I accepted that I would stay there for ten years. So I planned my daily life and determined to stay emotionally and physically strong until my ten years were over.

Beside depression, I suffered other illnesses and disease during the five years. One morning I woke up with a large lump in my throat. I raised this with the prison guard, and as the lump was big and noticeable, they took me the same day to the prison's clinic where the Ghezel Hesar doctor examined me. He couldn't diagnose the lump and referred me to the specialist in Evin Prison. I was told that the next day I would be transferred to Evin to see the specialist there. The prison guard told me that I would be brought back to Ghezel Hesar the same day.

When the lump appeared in my throat, a rush of thoughts came to my mind. I imagined that it was cancerous. What if I could never get out alive? I thought of my family, how much they had already suffered and how I should deliver the news to them. My friends were telling me that if it was dangerous, I might be released sooner than the end of my sentence.

The next day, I was blindfolded and transferred to Evin in a mini bus. From the time I left the ward until the mini bus left Ghezel Hesar, it took many hours, so that I arrived at Evin Prison late in the afternoon. The specialist doctor had finished work for the day, and I had to wait until the next morning. That night they took me into a single cell. It was dark and dirty, and the floor and walls were cement. The door was made of heavy metal, with a small window at the top. A toilet and a small basin were inside the cell. There was no bed and only one dirty blanket. We called those blankets patooye sarbazi, which means soldiers' blanket. These blankets were made from rough wool and they were dark grey. I tried to settle there and rest, with the blanket wrapped around me. I had my chador on. Suddenly, I woke up with a severe kidney pain. The pain was unbearable. I waited a while, thinking it would calm down. But it got worse. I remembered that when I was a child I had passed a kidney stone. The pain was the same. I was sure this time I was again passing a stone. When I couldn't bear the pain any longer, I started knocking at the door and asking the guards to get me a doctor. But there was no response. Finally, after two hours a prison guard came and opened the little window on the heavy metal door. She told me that no doctor was available at that time of the night, as it was after midnight. I asked her for a couple of strong pain killers. I told her that I had a history of kidney stones, explaining that pain killers will relax my muscles. That way I could pass the stone in my urine. Luckily, she listened to me and brought me a couple of pain killers. After an hour, the pain had gone. The next morning, I noticed that a tiny stone had passed.

In the morning they took me to the Evin clinic. After an x-ray, the specialist examined the lump in my throat and the result was negative, which meant that it was not a dangerous lump. I was told that it was a fatty tissue that would disappear on its own. After a few days, the lump totally disappeared.

Another health issue for me was a severe weakness in my right knee. When I was walking my knee would bend. I had no control over it. I suppose that lack of nutritious food, exercise and stress were the causes. All I could do was to buy honey and yoghurt and eat it mixed daily. I also tried to walk more in the ward. The problem persisted for a few months. I was not the only person with this knee problem, as a few other prisoners suffered from this health issue. It happened to me when I was in Ward 8, the Punishment Ward, where we did not have a yard in which to walk, nor was there any sunshine. The ward was much smaller than the other ward (Ward 4).

In the second year of my imprisonment they informed us that those with teeth problems could have treatment. One of the prisoners, who was a dentist, offered to fix other prisoners' teeth. I had four teeth which needed filling. She was highly expert in her job, and filled all my four teeth in one day. She did not use any anaesthetics, so it was painful. But the imprisonment and difficulties had made me resistant to suffering, and the pain was not as bad as the whipping. Nor was it as bad as the emotional torture we received on a daily basis.

Like many other prisoners, in general my health was okay. I was more resistant to the harsh condition than some other prisoners. They were the minority who could not bear the prison condition and became very depressed.

CHAPTER 12

Interrogation

During the third year of my imprisonment, in 1984, Ayatolah Montazeri was pressuring the authorities to release prisoners. As a result, he formed an Amnesty committee called komeiteye aff, to reopen and reinvestigate the prisoners' backgrounds with the aim to free or reduce the sentences of those prisoners who were less involved in political activities or were not politically active at all. The committee came from Evin Prison to Ghezel Hesar to reopen our files and investigate. A section in the prison outside of our ward, near the offices, was designated for this. It was a summer day. After the committee arrived and settled in, they started calling some of the prisoners' names for interview and interrogation. I was one of them.

I covered up in my chador and went to the door. The prison guard blindfolded us, and we were instructed to grab each other's tail (the back of the chador). Then in a long queue we started walking to the designated place. The person in the front held a stick that the prison guard was holding from the other end. It took a few minutes to get there. Once we arrived at the destination, we were seated on the floor of the corridor and waited for the interrogators to call us. Many things went through my mind. At that point I still had no idea what this was all about. Was I there to be punished for not repenting and becoming one of them? Or had someone reported my name again? My heart was beating fast! I was whispering some prayers. It was only later that we found out that the committee was formed by Ayatollah Montazeri with the aim of releasing prisoners. We then realised why the interrogators had not been rough with us.

After half an hour or so, one of the investigators called my name. I was taken to a separate room and told to sit on the floor. The floor was covered by carpet. Although I could not see the interrogator's face, the sound of his voice made me very uncomfortable. I felt helpless and exposed, as though he was looking at me as if I was naked. The investigation took about half an hour. First he asked for my name and other details, then started questioning me about the day of my arrest. He said to me that some of my friends had confessed and given my name as an active Mojahedin supporter. He told me that I could no longer hide the truth.

I could not deny my connection with Mojahedin as one of their supporters. Every detail concerning my activities and connections was discussed. I was still hesitant to reveal every detail, and confined my information to a brief admission. For example, I did not mention the different team houses where we gathered and had meetings. Luckily, he did not persist in finding every detail, and my 10-year sentence stayed unchanged.

The physical and emotional torture we received led some prisoners to confess, the result of persistent and animalistic persecution. I do not blame them for not being able to tolerate the torture. Different people have differing levels of resistance and tolerance. Their confession does not make them any less a person of character and determination. They believed in something and they fought for it. It is the fanatical Islamic government that must take responsibility and be sanctioned for torturing people for their beliefs.

As a result of these prisoners' confessions, my name and the names of other friends were recorded on the list of active Mojahedin supporters.

At the end of interrogation, we were sent to the ward. After a week or so, they announced by microphone the names of the prisoners in the ward whose sentences had been reduced or would end in the next few weeks. I was one of them. The reason that they did not increase my sentence could have been due to the time of my arrest on 30 Khordad 1360 (the Persian date for 20 June 1981), which was just before the start of Mojahedin underground activities. In addition, the committee's main agenda was to release prisoners. Otherwise, the result of this interrogation could have been worse. Basically, they did not reduce my sentence nor end my sentence, because I had confined my confession to my identity and not said anything about my activities at the time of my arrest.

CHAPTER 13

Release

Towards the middle of 1986, a sense of anticipation, tinged with fear, had been growing for a few weeks. Pressure on the government had been building strongly. Ayatolah Montazeri, the respected human rights activist and an Islamic democracy advocate, along with a number of international organisations, were putting the pressure on the government to release the prisoners. Some of the prisoners that were released and escaped from Iran had alerted those international organisations of the inhuman and animalistic behaviour of prison authorities against the prisoners. As a result, some of the prisoners were released before the end of their sentence. All of us wondered if and when we might be set free.

The hot summer day of 4 July started much like any other day. We were up early, the day shift organised breakfast and cleaned up, others got the hot water for cleaning, and by around 8 am most of us were walking around the corridors in twos or threes casually chatting. Then an announcement started on the loudspeakers. As was the usual response, we all stopped walking and talking to listen carefully to the booming voice. The announcement concerned a small number of prisoners who were to be released that day. At about the sixth of the eight names, my name was announced.

My heart was beating so fast as they asked us to pack our belongings and be ready for the next announcement to leave the ward. I started packing. My friends from the cell and other friends from the other cells all surrounded me. After packing, I hugged them and said goodbye; I was crying and laughing at the same time.

After one hour that they called our names. We went to the door. They blindfolded us and took us to a room in the prison where they took our photos and fingerprints. Meanwhile, our families were outside the prison, waiting for us since morning. They had been told of our imminent release a few days earlier, but had no way of letting us know – we remained in ignorance until the actual day of release. The authorities had not told the families the exact time when they would release us. Every time the door was opened, the families thought it was us getting out!

Finally, at about 1 pm on the hot summer afternoon of 4 July 1986, I was released from Ghelzelhesar Prison. They let us all out together. I looked around to find my family, and suddenly spied my father, my sister and my brother-in-law. My mum was at home preparing food so that when I got home, I could enjoy home-made food, the first for five years, one month and five days. We hugged and cried. My sister was very emotional. My father looked so happy. My brother-in-law was appointed as my guarantor.

I was happy and sad at the same time. Happy because I was getting out of that hell. I was going to be with my family members. The sad part of my freedom was that I was leaving behind a group of friends and five years of my life – I was used to and familiar with those friends and to some extent to that controlled lifestyle. Or at least I thought I had got used to it. Now I appreciate that this was due to the hidden depression that we all suffered. In prison we learnt to support each other. We learnt to compromise and be strong. Not that prison taught us these things; we taught ourselves to be more patient and persistent towards life. We learnt to care for each other and it became part of our nature. Otherwise life would have been too difficult to survive. No human nor any creature can be captive for such a long time without support.

I was free, and many things had changed since my arrest. My family had moved to another house, the new one having been under construction before my arrest. It was located in a beautiful new suburb called Shahrak Cheshme. The architecture of this little town was the responsibility of an Italian company which had a contract to finish it quickly. The houses were all double storied. After the revolution, though, the government released the Italian company and a local construction company took over the remaining work. It took forever for them to finalize the project. Finally, a year before my release, my family moved to the new house. My room was ready for me to go back home.

There were other major changes in my family's situation over the last five years. My eldest brother was married and had two beautiful children. My sister also had two beautiful daughters, of whom I met the elder one briefly once at the prison. Now I finally met the younger daughter as well. My little brother, who was only 12 years old at the time of my arrest, had now grown up and was studying at a college to become an electrician. He is the youngest and the smartest of all of us. My middle brother had left the country and was in Australia. He has two degrees, and a PhD in Physics. And my dear parents had grown older. They looked older than their age because of the stress that my imprisonment had caused them. Happily my release wiped some of the age lines from their faces, with friends and relatives telling me how they now looked ten years younger than before.

Yes, I had my freedom, though I had to report to the authorities about my daily activities. This freedom allowed me to rest whenever I liked, to read all types of books, novels, true stories, histories and so on, and I was freed to go to my relatives' homes, to visit my friends and feel free to speak. I did not have to worry all the time that I was under surveillance. I could see my parents every day and not worry and ask myself if they are okay. I could spend time with my nieces and nephews whenever I missed them. I could go to university and complete the course that I previously couldn't finish just because the government wanted to bring the so-called cultural revolution into the universities. So, they decided to close these centres where people go for intellectual developments and inner evolution.

I could also meet the friends I met in the prison who had been released before me. One of them was Nafise, very attractive and tall, with dark blonde curly hair. After release she came to my home. My other friend was Fariba, who was so kind and lovely. She wished for her brother to marry me. We saw each other a few times until one day, when I went to her house, her mother told me that she was not there and they didn't know where she was. I then realised that she has escaped the country. I never saw her again.

My best friend was Bahereh, whom I had known since my teenage years when we started our friendship at high school. We were so close that we would stay at each other's homes overnight. Any excuse was good reason for us to stay overnight. After study, we would lie on the bed and started chatting, joking, laughing, talking about boys, and talking about our future plans, until we couldn't keep our eyes open and fall asleep. After we finished high school, Bahereh and I applied to study in India. However, after the revolution, the embassy cancelled our visas and our plan was dashed. Bahereh started working and I entered the university. But we would still see each other at least two or three times a week. We would get together in the afternoon and meet in a beautiful park called Parke Lale. After my arrest, I lost contact with her, and even after my release I did not see her, but a few years ago we happily connected again through the social media.

During my detention, I did not know much about the outside environment. The changes that happened over the five-year period were huge. Before my arrest, political activities were still public. But since the arrests, everything had gone underground. I was anxious what life had for me now. I was anxious about what to expect at my weekly report to the authorities. I was beset by all these ambiguities.

But I was a lucky one. As it turned out, two years after my release, the authorities executed more than 4,500 prisoners who did not accept their Hezbollah ideology.

CHAPTER 14

First Day of Freedom

We arrived home around 1.30 pm. My father opened the door. I entered a house in which I had never lived. Our family house! It was a double story townhouse with a beautiful small garden and a pool with a few little red fishes swimming in it. In the garden my father had planted some colourful flowers and a few fruit trees, including a pomegranate and an apple tree. Every spring he would bring a gardener to help him with planting violets, dandelions and orchids. He would then maintain it himself. He loved gardening. The garden looked like a colourful painting created by an artist. My mum would sometimes assist by fertilizing the garden with tea leaves and fruit compost.

I walked into the house. There was a small corridor in the entrance, and on the floor was a dark brown carpet. A TV lounge was on the left. A large decorative Persian carpet was thrown in the middle of the TV lounge on top of the brown carpet. The carpet was from Tabriz, in the northwest of Iran.

My parents are from Tabriz, a city highly famed for its carpets. My mum had decorated the house elegantly. We still had our old furniture: a green three-seat sofa and four arm chairs. In one corner, Mum had placed a large indoor Bowiea Volubillis in a vase, which climbed the interior wall. The care for it is challenging, but my mother had a trick which worked well. She would fertilize it with a residue of tea leaves and fruits. Guests and visitors were amazed how she had managed to grow it so tall and green. On the right of the lounge was a dining table with six chairs. The kitchen was open, situated on the right side of the dining room. Across from the entrance was a toilet.

My father called my mum to announce that we were home. My mother rushed to the door and hugged and kissed me. Joyous tears wet our eyes. My youngest brother, Masoud, rushed down the stairs. We hugged. He had grown a lot. He was not a 12-year-old teenage boy anymore! Now he was a 17-year-old young man. I felt a sense of love, life and hope in me again. Nothing looked strange or unfamiliar to me. The smell and aroma of Mum's cooking brought back memories from the time I was at university! Every night after uni, I went home and we all sat on the floor around the Sofreh, a table cover we spread on the floor. The food was placed in the middle, and the family sat around it to have their meals. This was common with Persians. Using a Sofreh is a feature of Middle Eastern culture. Even later after we had a dining table, we loved sitting on the floor and having our meal around the Sofreh, especially when we had a large number of relatives and friends over for lunch and dinner. We would spread a long Sofreh from one end to the other end of the lounge room. Once the colourful food was put on the Sofreh, everyone sat around and helped themselves to the delicious feast.

After a very warm welcome from my mum and my brother, before lunch we sat in the lounge and Mum brought us tea. My dad helped her in the kitchen. We chatted about the day and how they waited for hours outside the prison! We talked about our relatives. However, I wasn't yet ready to meet any relatives. I needed to be alone to find myself. Five years in isolation had its impact on me. My family were very understanding and never pushed me into doing anything against my wishes. They never asked about those five years, one month and five days. And to date I have never told them.

During my incarceration I had lost a lot of weight, and was only 42 kilos when released from jail. I have a fair complexion, but my skin had become very dark. It took a couple of months for me to gain some weight and get my normal colour back. It was then that my sister confessed that she did not recognize me the first day. She cried a lot to herself, and worried about my health. She wondered if I could ever recover from that state I was in and whether I would ever look like the same joyful and happy person she had known again. I felt deep depression inside me. They felt it too, and tried to help me in their own way, partly by not asking me questions about my prison time so that I could get on with my life. I did not tell them either, as I knew that would make them anguished and sad.

It was around 3 pm that we sat around the table in the dining room and ate my mum's delicious food. Mum had made her signature dish, Zereshk polo ba Morgh, which is basmati saffron rice with chicken, garnished with Persian barberry. The love and affection from my family gave me a sense of security and comfort! During the five years I had many dreams at night seeing myself being at home, but before waking up would see myself returning to the jail. But now being at home with my family was so real and there wasn't any threat of return or sign for me to worry. There was nothing to take this happy feeling away from me. That was an amazing experience! From the warm welcome by my father, my mother, my sister, my little brother and my brother-in-law to the warm environment inside the home, and the delicious homemade food; it was all healing.

The jail food was just something to keep us alive. As well, they added camphor to it to squash the prisoners' sexual desires. That was their way of controlling such issues. The number of prisoners was too great for the size of the cells and the number of beds. As a consequence, in many cases two prisoners slept on a single bed. Being far from the family and loved ones, their needs and desires to love and be loved, and their hormonal changes could lead to sexual attraction. I always had self-respect and control over my desires and emotions.

After lunch, my family took me for a tour of the rest of the house. The entrance door looked onto wooden stairs leading to four bedrooms, a bathroom, an extra toilet and a storeroom on the second floor.

My room was opposite the stairs, with my bedroom door about two metres from the top of the stairs. Next to my bedroom there was a spare room which apparently used to be my youngest brother Masoud's room. He was now using the room opposite to mine, on the other side of the stairs. That room used to be my middle brother Amir's bedroom. Amir was in Australia, having escaped Iran two years prior to my release. He left Iran to avoid joining the national army. Back then there was a war between Iran and Iraq, and serving in the national army was compulsory for young males. Many of them lost their lives in this war. When he decided flee Iran and continue his education, my parents supported him and paid a people smuggler to help him escape.

My parents' bedroom was the one in the other corner opposite to mine. The bathroom, the second toilet and the storeroom were between my parent's bedroom and the spare room.

After the tour my sister and my brother-in-law went to their home and I went to my room to rest. The rest of the day I spent with my mum. My dad went to his small real-estate shop.

This was how I spent the first day out of the prison.

CHAPTER 15

Out of Prison but Not Free

I was free from prison, but elements of my ordeal continued. During the first year of my release, every Wednesday morning at 11am I was required to report to the Revolutionary Committee, the so-called Komiteye Enghelab. That day, from the moment I woke up, I felt anxious. I lay in bed thinking what was waiting for me? At the beginning my father would drive me there and, later on, I took a bus. On those days my heart was beating so fast, whilst I was commuting in the bus. I could hear the sound of my heartbeat and see my chest moving under the chador. Sometimes I felt I was about to throw up. Once I arrived, they would blindfold me and lead me to a room where I would sit on a chair. The officer, or so called Pasdar, would start the interrogation. Question after question, it went on and on, seeking details of my daily routine and my weekly activities. Had I met any new people? If yes, he would then ask me for the names and details. Had I visited any of my relatives? If yes, what was the subject of our conversation? Had there been any changes in my life? I had to give him every detail. I never mentioned the visits of my prison friends, Fariba and Nafise. There was a risk that they would take me back to the jail. This was one of the main reasons that I felt distressed and anxious. Plus, being blindfolded again brought back bad memories and created fear and uncertainty. After a year, they changed the arrangement, so that I then had to report every fortnight. This continued until the time I escaped the county.

Putting aside the reporting dilemma, it took couple of months for me to be ready to meet other people, including friends and relatives. For those two months I spent a lot of time in my room lying on my bed and reading books, including *War and Peace*, *The Desire* and *Gone With the Wind*, among other historical romance pieces. My sister almost every day came to see me. Occasionally I went to her house to spend time with my gorgeous nieces, Ghazaleh and Maral. Some nights I slept over. Helping my sister with her children was very healing. They were demanding like many other kids and that kept me busy. Being with them was a distraction from my thoughts and nightmares of the jail. They made me happy. My sister sometimes left the kids with me and went to do her daily banking and shopping. I helped my nieces with their studies, fed them, cleaned them, played with them and even made dresses for them.

Many times, my father asked me to drive the car to my sister's home instead of taking public transport or asking for a lift. I had lost so much confidence that I didn't touch the car for three years. I was terrified to drive. The only place that I drove was to my sister who was only 10 minutes' drive from our house.

Before my eldest brother, Hossein, moved from Tonkabon in Noshahr (in the north of Iran) to Tehran, I drove with my mother and father to Tonkabon to visit them. It is a fair distance, taking about seven hours. Cities in the north of Iran are popular holiday destinations, due to their geographic situation, the weather and being surrounded by the Caspian Sea. This was the first time after my release that I saw my eldest brother and his family. And for the first time, I met my handsome little nephew, Ali, and my beautiful little niece, Solmaz.

The roads to Tonkabon are extremely hazardous, being very narrow and winding. On one side of the road there are tall rocky hills and the other side a deep valley. Whist we were driving, it felt like the rocks were leaning towards us, so close that we could touch them, and for the other side of the road, it felt that we would fall down the valley. Going through all this excitement and danger was perhaps worth it, as the region is one of the most striking natural wonders of the world. The scenery surrounding it is incredibly beautiful, like painted green velvet.

Three years after my release, Hossein moved to Tehran with his family. This gave me a chance to see him and his family more often. Overall though, I was closer to my sister.

Almost every Friday, all the family would come to us. Four children, my three nieces and one nephew, would mix well and play together. The kids loved climbing the stairs, playing hide and seek, chasing each other up and down, fighting and becoming friends again. You could hear them scream, laugh, run and jump. You could see their joy of being with their grandma and grandpa and having freedom to play. After I left Iran, my siblings had even more children.

Every morning, I would usually get up early and join my father, who was the first to rise. This was my habit from childhood, to be awake and ready for the day. I am still the same. By the time I went downstairs, he was up and ready. Each morning in summer, he first watered the garden (which I also loved doing), then bought freshly baked bread and a daily newspaper from close-by local shops. He then made the tea and sat sipping it while he read the paper. We then waited for my mum to wake up and join us for breakfast together. This typically consisted of Panire Tabrizi (feta cheese from Tabriz), butter with honey or jam, boiled eggs, and fresh cream with Persian style bread, Noon Sangak, Lavash, Barbary or Taftoon. I still crave for those days. After breakfast I helped my mum with everyday house cleaning.

My mum is very keen on cleaning. Every year, a couple of weeks before the spring, we had major spring cleaning, everything from washing the carpets to dusting, cleaning the cobwebs, cleaning the windows and washing the floors. The highlight of spring cleaning is 'Nowruz', meaning 'New day', this being our New Year celebration. It starts from 1st Farvardin, usually 21 March each year, with the setting of a colourful 'haft seen' table, wearing new outfits, visiting family and friends, wishing each other prosperity and success and giving each other gifts. The last day of celebration is 13 Farvardin, 3 April, when everyone goes out for a picnic to end the Nowruz. 'Haft seen' means 'seven seen', and 'seen' is part of the alphabet in the Persian language. We have seven items on our tables with the starting letter of 'seen'. The most common items starting with the letter 'seen' are: 'Sabzeh' (wheat, barley or lentil sprouts grown in a dish) which is the symbol of rebirth; 'Samanu' (a sweet pudding made of wheat germ), a symbol of affluence; 'Senjed' (dried fruit of the oleaster tree), symbol of love; 'Seer' (garlic), the symbol of medicine; 'Seeb' (apple), which stands for beauty and health; 'Somag' (Sumac), the symbol of sunrise; and 'Serkeh' (vinegar), a symbol of age and patience. Other popular items are 'Sonbol' (hyacinth flower), the symbol of spring and finally 'Sekeh' (coins), symbols of prosperity and wealth.

Two months after my release, my mother organised a welcome party for me. Beside my siblings with their families, she invited my aunties, uncles and cousins from both sides of the family. By then many of my other relatives had left the country for overseas, scattered all over the world: America,

Sweden, UK, Germany, Australia, Canada and others. The revolution separated families, relatives and friends. That day, however, the house was full, with everybody chatting and mingling. My mother was busy in the kitchen, with my sister and sister-in-law helping. My aunties Roghi and Marzi were also assisting. My mother is a fantastic cook, and made her signature dish that day: Zereshk polo ba morgh (chicken with rice garnished with saffron and Persian Barberry). She cooked many other foods as well. Everyone was happy to see me alive. I could see and feel they were all curious to know what happened to me in the jail, but no one allowed themselves to ask about my time in prison. I was happy and thankful for that. I did not want to put myself in danger, as I had to report everything to the authority. I could have been under surveillance and if I lied that could have changed everything. Plus, I was very shy back then and not very talkative. Time has changed me a lot and I am glad who I am now.

Reading, chatting to our neighbours, visiting friends and relatives, and spending time with my siblings was part of my day to day activities. Except for my sister's home, if it was anywhere else, I went with my family.

Fariba, one of my jail-time friends, was the only one who I visited at her home. We started by phoning each other. She had hoped that her brother, a doctor, would marry me. Fariba's younger brother was married to a friend of mine, Zari, something we discovered when we both were still in jail. Zari and Fariba invited me and my mother to their home, a big two-level house where they were all living. Fariba with her parents and older brother were living on the first floor, and Zari with her husband and child were living on the second floor. It was the last month of summer, a month after my release, that we went to visit them. After that she became my best friend, and our families were close. I would call her almost every day, until after a year or so, every time I called to talk to her, her mother said that she wasn't home. My sixth sense told me that

Fariba had left the country. Then, one day when I called again and asked to speak to her, her mother invited us over, and it was confirmed Fariba had left Iran! From then until now, I have never seen or heard anything about her again.

Fariba's brother did not propose to me, as I think he had a girlfriend. I don't recall his name, though I remember his face and appearance. He wasn't a tall man and he was a bit chubby. I didn't mind him, but he was not handsome. I suppose that he being a doctor made him attractive in my eyes. There was pressure from my family for me to get married. Plus, there was pressure to marry a doctor or an engineer in our culture. The thought of marrying a doctor or an engineer had become almost every girl's dream.

Over those four years, many men proposed to me, but I wasn't interested. Except one. It was love at first sight for me. Only a month of my freedom had passed when he and his mother came to our house to see me. He was the nephew of the husband of a family friend who introduced us to each other. I was still very skinny. He was tall and extremely handsome, with dark hair and green eyes. He was an engineer too! He was wearing a white shirt with black trousers. His mother, however, would not allow our relationship to develop, because in her eyes we were not rich enough. For example, we didn't have luxurious furniture at home. I remember spending a few days in bed with fever, and crying a lot, though I hid this from my family. Every day for next few days I asked my mum if she heard anything from them, but there was nothing. Four years later, one month before I fled Iran, we met the mother at our friend's house. That night, I had my hair done in a big wave, and was wearing a black blouse tucked into a grey, stylish midi skirt. I had make-up on and was looking beautiful. She looked at me eagerly with smile. I knew she was very regretful and sorry, especially when she found out that I was cousin to a rich and wealthy family in Tabriz. Meanwhile, her son had married his cousin. The only thing I could think of that night was that I must leave my country. I could not wait any longer.

Nafise was the other friend from the jail whom I kept in contact with after the release. She was an attractive young woman; tall, with dark blonde curly hair and an athletic slim appearance. Nafise was very classy. She came once to my home, and we kept in contact by calling each other regularly until I left the country. I couldn't say goodbye to her, as no one knew that my youngest brother and I were leaving the country. We even hid it from my sister and brother-in-law. Only my mother, my father and my eldest brother, Hossein knew. Hossein drove us to Salmas, on the border of Iran and Turkey. From there we surrendered into the hands of people smugglers, an experience I describe in the next chapter.

Other highlights of my life during those four years included the completion of my Associate Diploma in Accounting. The universities, after the educational revolution, had re-opened with some major changes whilst I was still in the jail. Our uni was designated for girls only, and the boys were moved to another centre. After my release I decided to finish my studies, which took a bit over a year to complete. I also worked for a short period for a company doing bookkeeping, though I still wasn't ready to go out in public – I had no confidence in myself. Plus, I didn't approve of the manager's behaviour with his staff. I found him to be a rude and inconsiderate person. He was planning to fire one of his employees and give me the job. I felt for the employee, as he was a family man with children. These two things together convinced me to refuse the job. I also helped my brother-in-law, a successful professional accountant, with his work at home, which he paid me for doing the work.

CHAPTER 16

Escape from Iran

Four years passed. My mother was concerned that government forces would arrest me again. During the months of Ashora and Tasooa (Arabic calendar – Hijri), members of Hezbollah would march on the street to show their sorrow for historical incidents concerning Moslem leaders more than 1,400 years ago. During those months, every time Hezbollah forces passed our house, my mother worried that they might come to our house and take me away. My parents frequently discussed ways to help me flee Iran. By then I was ready to leave the country. We focused on finding out if there was a way for me to flee Iran by air. I spoke to my friend Nafise, who had been released a year earlier than me, to check if she had been able to get a passport. She had been unsuccessful, even though her sentence had been completed before her release. As my sentence of 10 years still hadn't been completed, there was no way to obtain a passport. I wasn't sure what was going to happen to me!

Masoud, my youngest brother, was studying to be an Electrician in a TAFE. The war between Iran and Iraq was still happening, meaning he would soon have to join the army. Many young soldiers were killed or declared missing during this war. We were worried that if Masoud joined the army, he could become another casualty. We tried to convince him to flee the country, along with me.

My father turned his attention to finding people smugglers to help us. Contrary to Western perspectives, people in Iran have different views about people smugglers. We look at them as a channel of escape. It is impossible to escape the borders without their help. They were our source and hope of freedom. One day my father came home and said that he has found some Kurdish people to help me and Masoud to flee the country. He was assured that they were very trustworthy people. Kurds are well known as fighters and warriors, having fought for decades to gain freedom and independence. They are very kind and welcoming people and not particularly religious. The majority of them are Sunni.

My father invited them to our house. Two Kurds came, and my parents had a long conversation with them. They talked about the safety of the way, along with the price and the duration. My parents asked how they could trust them? The Kurds responded by explaining that when my parents took us to the meeting place in Salmas, they would meet their family and know of their whereabouts. Once my mother and father felt happy, they set the date for my brother and I to go to their home in Salmas. They asked us not to talk to anyone about the plan, otherwise word could spread and put us all in danger. One week from that day, we would set off.

No one, no friends nor most family members knew that Masoud and I were going to flee the country. The plan was that Masoud and I would be driven to the Kurds' house in Salmas, from where our dangerous trip would start. They told my parents to take us there at 10 pm.

When my parents started to plan, they decided to tell my eldest brother Hossein. We needed his help to drive us to Salmas, in northwest Iran. It was a long drive, about 10 to 12 hours, during which we had to pass government security checkpoints. My mother and I were wearing black chadors to disguise ourselves as Hezbollah supporters. As a precaution we took one small luggage each, carrying the necessities or otherwise it would have drawn attention to us if we were stopped. In addition, we had to move fast and carrying suitcases would have slowed us down. We had some clothing and shoes, as well as basic care products such as shampoo, soap, tooth brushes and tooth paste. My luggage included some photos and documents from my jail time.

A few hours into our journey, just before Rezaeieh (old Urmia), security forces stopped us. We had already passed a few of them, and this was the only one that stopped us. They asked where we were from and where was our destination? My mother, Masoud and I were sitting in the back passengers' seat. My father was in the front and Hossein was driving. Hossein, in a very calm and confident manner, told the security forces that my mother had arthritis in her legs and were going to Rezaeieh for a holiday and to use the mud from the lake. The mud from Rezaeieh's lake is well known for its curing properties for such pains. My mother in the back seat was whispering some prayers. I was also praying. Conditions of my release from jail meant that I was not allowed to go anywhere out of Tehran, the capital city, especially without informing them. My heart was beating very fast. The security guard looked into our faces one by one. He also checked my brother's driving license. He pretended to be very calm, though I could see the anxiety and worry in his face.

I suppose my brother's calmness and my mother's prayers helped us to pass this point safely. We had a short break in Rezaeieh, where we stopped in a park and had some food that my mother had prepared for our way. She had made Kotlet

(Beef Patty) sandwiches. It was summer and the days were hot and long. After our brief stop, we left Rezaeieh for Salmas, a short distance further. Back then there was no GPS. If you were not using a map, you would ask people for the address. Getting to Rezaeieh (Urmia) was easy for my brother, as he spent a year of his national army service there. He was a driver for one of the Generals and knew the area well. However, he still needed to ask some locals for final directions.

From Rezaeieh to Salmas was about one and a half hours' drive. It was around 9.30 or 10 at night when we arrived. Once there, it was easy to find the Kurds' address with the directions we'd been given by the locals. When we arrived, the Kurds and their family were waiting for us, and invited us into the house. The house was in a wood. It was made of clay. My parents wanted to meet the family, and asked some questions to make sure of our safety. We sat on the floor, and they spread a Sofreh and offered us some food. I was anxious, as I didn't know what was waiting for us.

Towards midnight, my parents and my eldest brother said goodbye and we all went out. There were a couple of brown horses waiting for us in the woods. They were huge! Two Kurds were with us leading the horses along the way. We sat on the back of the horses, holding the riders from the waist, passing through the woods for a couple of hours. Once we arrived at the rocky hills, the horses couldn't carry two people. The Kurds got off, walking the horses and holding the straps. We kept going all night. In the morning we sheltered for breakfast and rested behind some rocks under the trees. It was around 6.30 am, and the Kurds gave us bread, feta cheese and herbs. That was our food for the trip most of the way. Luckily the weather was very pleasant. By this stage I was wearing a scarf, jeans and a cream-coloured Czech Manto.

After couple of hours, we moved on. The Kurds had many friends who went ahead of us to check the way and give the green signal. If the roads were not safe, they would change directions. It was around 1 in the afternoon that we arrived at another safe place on top of the hills. One of the Kurds went to the village and brought us warm food, Kebab with bread. After lunch, we rested there until the night, then continued moving. Nights were safer for travel as there was not any light. Our guides used the moon's light for direction.

The next day we arrived at a house where we rested until sunset and had to leave. By the third night we were exhausted, having moved throughout the whole night. In the early morning, around 2 am, the Kurds become more alert, as we were about to pass the Iranian border into Turkey. We stopped and one of the Kurds went ahead to check the way. After 15 minutes or so, he came back and directed us through this dangerous area. After couple of hours, the Kurds told us that we were safely in Turkey.

We were taken to a mud house on top of a hill in a village in Kurdistan. The family who lived there did not have any running water, using the water from a well for their daily consumption. Their living conditions were primitive, as the electricity wasn't working and there was no proper toilet. The family included a teenage girl and a young boy, and they all wore traditional Kurdish clothing. For the last few days we had been continually moving with no chance to have a shower and refresh ourselves. Finally I could wash, and the lovely teenage girl poured warm water on my head to help clean my hair. My brother did the same. We stayed the whole day in their house with these very kind people, who fed us lunch and dinner of boiled meat with rice.

At sunset we had to leave again, this time led by the Kurd from the house. We set off along a dangerous path, moving very fast, almost running. Turkish security forces were everywhere. For decades, clashes between Kurds and the Turkish government have continued, as the Kurds seek their independence. Because of that, Turkish government forces were present everywhere, maintaining surveillance and control. As well, the Iranian government knew that freed political prisoners and others who were opposed to the Islamic regime would try to escape across the border into Turkey. It was the only path and we had to get through it.

I saw a farmer tending his sheep and goats at a stable who was looking at us. I brought it to the Kurd's attention, but he reassured us that it was fine. Around 10 that night we reached a road. Masoud continued part of the way on foot with the Kurd. I was separated from him and led to a white utility waiting for me. I got into the car, and after 10 minutes' drive we picked up Masoud and the Kurd, who had used a short cut. We were in the car for quite a long time, about six hours or so. Early the next morning, towards sunrise, we arrived at a house in Van, a city in Eastern Turkey located on the shore of Lake Van. A large and very friendly family were living in that house. As we all knew the Azari language, we were able to communicate with each other. There are similarities between the Azari and Istanbul Turkish languages, which is why I could pick up their language easily. In fact, once we became official United Nations' refugees, I was used as an interpreter for other Persians who were new and did not understand Istanbul Turkish.

We stayed at that house the whole day. At night we had to leave for our final destination in Ankara. I had to disguise myself in a blue Kurdish dress. They also gave me a Kurdish birth certificate, which belonged to a young girl. We travelled by bus, and I sat in the back row with the Kurd, who pretended to be my father. Masoud, wearing a blue shirt, was sitting in the front row and chatting to the driver. Apparently, the driver knew that I was running away from my country, Iran. But he did not know that Masoud was my brother who was also running away. After two or three hours, the driver abruptly stopped the bus. The Kurd gave me the Kurdish birth certificate and told me that if anyone came to check on me, to show it to them. He then went to see what was happening, and talked to the driver. A few security guards were checking the bus, as it was an official checkpoint. We were there for almost an hour, and naturally I started worrying. I imagined that the security forces had somehow come to know about us. Eventually the Kurd came back and sat next to me, and reassured me that everything was fine. But I was scared, as I couldn't communicate well and didn't want to make anyone suspicious with my accent. Later on, I discovered that the driver found out that Masoud was also with me, and wanted more money to let Masoud travel in the bus. Finally they came to an agreement, and from then on Masoud pretended to be the driver's assistant. With added resting times, the trip took about 22 hours.

Thus, after two nights and a day, we arrived in Ankara at around 8 or 9 in the morning. Luckily, a friend of my father's, Mr Ataeyan, who was living in Ankara at the time, came to the bus station to meet us. Otherwise, we would not have known how to get around. He took us to the house where he was renting a room. We were also able to retrieve our luggage, which had travelled separately on a bus under the care of the Kurds.

CHAPTER 17

Ten Months in Turkey

The owner of the house was a very nice man named Hamid, from Tabriz in Iran. He looked well educated and behaved as a gentleman. He was very welcoming, showing us to a room where we put our luggage. We then joined him and my father's friend, Mr Ataeyan, in the lounge room. After relaxing for an hour or so, I asked if I could have a shower. My head itched, which I thought was due to the lack of washing for the past few days. But, even after regular washing, the itching remained. I then assumed it was due to changed weather condition. This highly uncomfortable itchy head persisted for about four months.

The day after our arrival in Ankara, we were given the United Nation's office address by Hamid and went there to apply for refugee status. Using a map of the city which Hamid gave us, we caught a bus to get there. At the door, a clerk gave us a number. Whilst we were waiting to be called, we met other refugees. One of them, Mohsen, was very helpful and asked about our background. I briefly told him about my political involvement and my imprisonment. I also told him how I was still required to report to the government before fleeing to Turkey. He suggested that I should stress this aspect of my personal history, even to exaggerate, in the interview in order to obtain refugee status. If we failed to convince them, they even might deport us to Iran. I was so scared, as I knew that if I went back to Iran there was a strong possibility that I would be executed.

My fear was highly justified. Two years after my release, all my friends in prison were killed in a massacre. This is now a matter of recorded history, when in 1988 the Iranian regime executed thousands of political prisoners. As summarized by Amnesty International, during the course of several weeks between late July and early September 1988, thousands of political dissidents were systematically subjected to enforced disappearance in Iranian detention facilities across the country and extrajudicially executed pursuant to an order issued by the Supreme Leader of Iran implemented across prisons in the country. Many of those killed were subjected to torture and other cruel, inhuman and degrading treatment or punishment in the process.[3]

That day we did the initial interview. They just took our name and address, and asked us if we had a passport or entered the country illegally. We were then given an appointment for the next week for a second interview with a United Nation's counsellor. Before the interview, we met our new friend a couple of times in a park. He helped us to prepare for our interview, giving us some of the questions that might come up. He also stressed that everything each of us said had to be consistent with each other. If there was any inconsistency, they

3 - https://www.amnesty.org/download/Documents/
MDE1394212018ENGLISH.PDF

would reject our application. During these meetings, we had question and answer sessions. He also gave us homework to practice every day so that we would be ready for the interview.

Mohsen was politically left wing, and was going to Canada. His fiancé, a Mojahedin supporter, was already living in Canada as a refugee. They had met in Ankara. Mohsen had also received Canadian refugee status. He was waiting for his final administration procedures to be completed.

The next week, the interview was conducted by a UN counsellor. She was probably from India, with dark hair and dark olive skin. We felt that the interview went well; I was confident about my background details, and we believed we would be accepted.

In Turkey, Masoud had a friend Ahmad who was also a refugee. He was a dark, tall, good looking young man who was living in a city called Chrome. Two weeks after our arrival to Turkey, he came to visit us. We had many questions about the refugees in Turkey. He was quite helpful, and stayed with us for a couple of days. He knew Ankara well, taking us around the city and checking out some open markets and shops. Ankara is a modern city, with many universities. After the revolution, many Iranians travelled there on student visas. Ahmad invited us to visit Chrome, but we would need permission from the police before going there. At our next reporting day to the police, we asked for permission to go there, explaining that we wanted to visit a friend. The next day we travelled there by bus, taking a few hours. Almost everyone in the bus was smoking, as back then smoking was not banned in public transport. Many people in Turkey start smoking from a very young age. I was coughing the whole time, unable to breathe properly, but I had no option.

The city was very nice and clean, but because of our meagre budget we were not able to do much. We stayed with Masoud's friend for few days. He told us that after couple of months the police would transfer us to another city. I believe they were trying to ensure that the refugees didn't overrun the capital city, as everyday new groups of people like us would come to Ankara. Too many refugees in Ankara would not have been good for the economy. Whilst we were there, Ahmad introduced us to one of his friends who had close contact with Mojahedin. I was hoping that his friend could assist us to get a letter of support from Mojahedin to help us obtain our refugee status. He assured us he would talk to his connection and pass on my request. He told us that the support letter would go direct to the UN head office in Ankara. I needed this letter to establish my refugee status on the basis of my political background and imprisonment.

Occasionally, we went to United Nation's office and waited outside to meet new refugees. On one of those visits we met some Mojahedin supporters who took us to their house, on a hilly suburb far from the city. Most of the buildings were four or five level apartments. Our new friends were living on the second floor of one of those buildings, in a two-bedroom apartment with about five people sharing. They were all from Iran, with two of them students and the other three refugees. We were served tea and dates, and we discussed Mojahedin, particularly their new moves and activities. I asked them for a support letter from the Mojahedin head authority to present to the UN, giving them my details to pass on.

At that time Mojahedin were based in a city in Iraq, close to the Iranian border, and there were sporadic clashes between them and the Iranian army. I was no longer interested in becoming politically involved with any kind of ideology again. My vision was to go to a third country and start a new life, far from all the politics and the complications. I wanted to go to university, get my degree and start a corporate job. I wanted to fall in love, get married, have children and enjoy life. So, I did not show any interest in joining them again, though I could see that they were trying to get me on board. We left after couple of hours, and we did not contact them or hear from them again. I had never regretted my past, my time in the jail or my previous involvement with Mojahedin, but by then I wanted something different from life.

Two months passed, while we waited for the UN's response. Once a week we went to the UN offices to check if a decision had been made. It was also our weekly schedule to go to the police, who informed us that our time in Ankara was over and we had to move to Nevsehir. We were given a letter with our details and photo identity to hand to the Nevsehir police. We had to pack quickly and leave Ankara the next day. We gave the news to Mr Ataeyan and to Hamid, and after a short rest started packing.

The next morning, we went to the police station for the last time. A policeman accompanied us to the bus station. They did this with everyone to make sure we went to the designated city. We were told to go to the police in Nevsehir on our arrival and give them the letter. We met a few Iranians on the bus who were in the same situation as us. All of us were to stay in Nevsehir until our refugee status was decided. Nevsehir, formerly Neapolis and Muşkara, is a city and the capital district of Nevsehir Province in the Central Anatolia Region of Turkey. A tourist city, it has many historical sites that visitors are very keen to see. One of them is an underground city, forming multiple levels beneath the earth. It had many tunnels and rooms, and is surprisingly interesting.

We left Ankara around 9 am, taking about four hours to arrive at the city centre in Nevsehir. After collecting our luggage we headed to the police station, where the police were waiting for us. None of the refugees who arrived there with us knew Turkish. I started talking in Azari to the police officer, who was impressed and asked me to interpret for them. I was happy to help my friends. The police briefly interviewed everyone, and I got special treatment, being given tea and biscuits. After taking all of our details and finger prints, they let us leave the station.

We had no place to go. We were told that we needed to look for a place ourselves. Nevsehir was very different from Ankara, being not as advanced nor as modern. In some areas, the streets were still not asphalted, and the houses were basic in structure. There were about a dozen of us, and we divided into groups of four, going street to street and knocking at doors, asking to rent a room. Some of us were joking loudly whilst walking through streets, asking if anyone had a room or house to rent. It was getting dark and we were all hungry and tired, still looking for a place to stay the night. Finally, we knocked at a door and an Iranian man answered. We were over the moon. He invited us into the house, where five people were living in three rooms.

It was the end of autumn and the weather was getting cold, but inside the house was pleasantly warm as they had heaters on. Later on, we discovered that they utilized the street power to warm up the inside of the house, as living expenses were very expensive. The landlord lived at the top level, and every time he went to check on the tenants, they would turn off the heaters and hide them. They did that to survive the cold winter there. That night we stayed with them. The next morning one of the guys from the house told me and Masoud that there was a young family, a husband and a wife with two children (a girl and a boy) who might be happy to have us in their house until we find another place. We went and introduced ourselves, explaining how we got their details. They invited us to their house, and were happy for us to stay with them until we found alternative accommodation. The husband had a PhD in history or social science – they called him Doctor. The wife was also an academic. They had left Iran to provide a better life for their children. Most of the refugees were academics or were planning to go to another country not only to have freedom but also to study.

We stayed with this young family for a month or so, and then moved to another place on the other side of the city to live with another lovely couple. They were newly married. The husband was Iranian and the wife was from Turkey. He was waiting to get his visa for one of the Scandinavian countries. Soon after we moved in, after one month, they received their visa, so we had to find another place. We still had contact with our friends from the other side of the city, as Masoud had kept contact with them. His friends told him that there was a room available for rent in the old area we lived before. All our friends were still on the other side of the city. Every night, we gathered in one of our friend's houses, spread a long Sofreh and shared our food, played cards, played Gol ya Pooch (a Persian play game), and made jokes. When we'd been on the other side of the city, the distance was too far and we hadn't been able to join our friends. Finding a new place near our friends made us very happy.

This time we moved in with two Iranians, Amir and Mohammad, as two of their housemates had received their visas from a third country and left Turkey. They were looking for replacements. Living in groups of four or five people in a house was a common pattern. Most of us did not have jobs and we were living on the small amount of money that we were receiving from the United Nations. Only those who had received their refugee status received money from UN. I was lucky that Masoud was with me. Soon after arriving at Nevshir, he found a job in construction. I also found a job, in a glass factory. The job was easy, but any time I sat to take a break, the manager objected, even if there was nothing to do. My feet would get tired very quickly and I now know that was due to my flat feet. I was not expecting this sort of treatment from the boss. My effort to enlighten him that if I was sitting when there wasn't any work around would not impact anyone or anything was pointless. I was fired the same day. I took my money and left. That was my one day of work in Turkey.

Every month, my parents sent us some money, about $100 US. They had to change their currency to US dollars, which had become very expensive. In addition, my mother came to visit us twice and each time she brought us lots of food, from rice, dry beans, dry soya, and dry herbs to cans of tuna. I was really thankful for all their support, which was a great help. We could not afford to buy meat, so I would go to the butcher and buy bone marrow and use it in casserole dishes in place of meat. It made the food tasty. In those days, bone marrow was very cheap. Once a month we treated ourselves to Turkish sausages, which in my opinion are the best.

Three months had already passed from the time we arrived in Nevsehir, and we still didn't know the outcome of our interview. I kept going to the police to check if they had received a letter or telegram from the UN. Back then communication was via letter and, in case of emergency, a telegram. Finally, one day when I went to the police, they gave me a telegram from the UN. Our first interview had been unsuccessful. However, in the telegram they invited us for a second interview. I was very disappointed with the outcome. The telegram didn't give any reason for our rejection. Later on I found out that the councillor had been transferred to another country. The second interview was in couple of days, so we bought tickets and went to Ankara. We stayed the night with Mr Ataeyan, my father's friend. The next morning, at around 8.30 am, we left there for the UN office. My heart was pounding.

Our interview this time was with a councillor from Holland. Everyone told us that he was very unbiased in his view, with strong intuition and an ability to distinguish the truths from lies. The time arrived and I was the first to be seen. We were separately interviewed. He was tremendously calm and kind, which gave me some assurance and relief. I could tell that he had studied our previous interview. The questions were around our reasons for escape, my political activities, my jail time, the way we fled, the outcome of my return to Iran, Masoud's reason to flee and his connection to my political activity and so on. It took more than one hour. I didn't know what to expect anymore. The next day, we went back to Nevsehir, where we were still living with Mohammad and Amir. This was our last home before we left for Australia.

One month passed. I was keen to know what the outcome would be this time. Mohammad, our flat mate, had gone to Ankara, as he sometimes went there to catch up with a friend. He also had a few friends working in the UN. I had a big crush on him, and believe he had one for me too. I was thinking about him and missing him. It was winter, and I was cleaning the house. Suddenly I heard someone call me from behind. I was startled and jumped. It was him – tall, broad shouldered, handsome Mohammad. He had shaved his moustache, and looked even more handsome. He said hi, and I replied that I wasn't expecting him to be back soon. He smiled at me and said he had good news. I couldn't wait to hear it! 'What is it?', I said. Then he gave me the good news – we'd been accepted by the UN! I wanted to hug him, but I didn't! I wish I could turn back time and tell him how I felt about him. I was too shy to express my feelings back then. I don't know why he never told me how he felt for me! Life has taught me a lot.

The next day we went to the police station to receive the official answer. This letter recognised our refugee status. To be eligible for UN financial support, we had to go to the UN office in Ankara again. After filling in the required form, the next day I returned to Nevsehir. The money was a small amount, but helped us to manage our life. My parents still sent us money from time to time, and Massoud was still working.

Once our refugee status was established, we waited to receive an interview with a third country. Refugees who had family in another country had a better chance to get accepted by that country's embassy. In addition, the UN expected us to ask our family members in other countries to send us a sponsorship visa, as this speeded up the immigration process. The ones who did not have family members or friends in other country waited long time to obtain visas. We had Amir, my middle brother, who had been living in Australia for six years. We applied to emigrate to Australia and waited for Amir to send us the sponsorship. The UN had already sent our case to the Australian embassy. Seven months from the time we landed in Turkey had passed.

We received our invitation for interview at the Australian embassy in Ankara. The interview took a few hours. During the interview, they also organised a course for us. They played a video in English, which briefly outlined information about Australia and the official process we would follow once we arrived. I could understand only about 40 percent of it. Even though we were refugees, since Amir was living in Australia, we were asked to pay for our own tickets. We were surprised, and Masoud argued with them about it. Because of this, our visa was delayed by three months. The day the visa arrived, we had only two weeks to leave Turkey. Amir and my parents supported us again with the necessary funds.

My connection to Mohammad was very strong. One day I was sleeping in my room and he was sleeping in his. A few friends were in the hall chatting, and they heard me talking in my sleep. I asked a question and he responded to it.

Another indication that he liked me was from the signs he showed and his reactions towards me. One evening Mohammad and I were going back home from one of the dinner parties we had almost every night. It was a wintery cold night, and everything was white and covered with snow. I was shivering, so Mohammad took off his jacket and put it around my shoulders. I asked him, 'What about you?' He said that he was fine! I was highly tempted to hug and hold him tight, and tell him how I felt about him. But my shyness stopped me. We were taught to resist our passions, and that men had to take the first step.

Mohammad received his refugee visa and left Turkey for Canada one month before me and Masoud. The day he went to tell the police about his visa, I was with him. The police officer asked him why he didn't take me with him to Canada? He looked at me, smiling, and my face turned red. We both kept quiet.

Mr Ataeyan, my father's friend, who was about 27 years my senior, liked me too. He was a very handsome man; slim, with some greys around his ears. I never imagined he had special affection for me, until one day he came to Nevsehir to visit us, and told me. My mum was visiting us at that time. He had bought a beautiful watch for me. I then realised his intentions but didn't have that kind of attraction towards him. I was thinking only about Mohammad. He insisted that I take the watch and gave me a little booklet in which he had written poems about me. He said that I inspired him to write them.

CHAPTER 18

Finally, Australia!

Two weeks were left before we would leave Turkey for Australia. I was excited. Amir booked two tickets for a flight from Istanbul with Alitalia.

Some of our friends had already left for a third country. Some went to the USA, some to Scandinavian countries, some to Canada and some were still waiting for their refugee status to be approved by the United Nations. We were the lucky ones, as we were in Turkey for only ten months, due to our strong case. There were others who were there for more than a year and were still waiting for the UN's response.

The two weeks passed quickly. My mum came to Nevsehir to say goodbye. We bought bus tickets to Istanbul. The day we had to leave, we said goodbye to my mum and our friends, who all came to the bus terminal. A police officer accompanied us to Ataturk airport in Istanbul. The bus left Nevsehir at 10 pm for the long drive of at least 10 hours. It was mid-morning when we arrived at the beautiful city of Istanbul. From the bus terminal, we caught a taxi to the airport, which took another hour.

On the way to Istanbul, the bus stopped to drop a few passengers, who picked their bags from the luggage department and left. I was anxious and wanting to get to Istanbul as soon as possible. More than half an hour passed and the bus still wasn't moving. It was then that we discovered that the policeman's bag had mistakenly been taken by one of the passengers at an earlier stop. The policeman who was accompanying us was outside talking to the bus driver. After about two hours, the bus left for Istanbul. We didn't find out what happened to his bag.

The policeman kept asking for money. We gave him a bottle of wine but refused to hand over any money. He kept insisting on money from us, and Masoud repeatedly told him that we didn't have any money. In Turkey, bribery was very common.

At the airport, we had another complication at the check-in desk. We had only travel documents. The administrative officer kept asking for passports and refusing to give us boarding passes. The policeman explained to her that we were UN refugees, with no passports. After multiple phone calls, she let us check-in our bags. Once the checking was done, we spent a few hours in transit. The flight finally departed at 10.45 pm. The plane passed over the Tehran sky, and after many hours we had a few hours stop at Singapore Airport. Then the plane left for Sydney where we stayed in the airport for a couple of hours before the final leg to Melbourne with Qantas. Again there were complications. Our luggage did not arrive, as it had been unloaded in Singapore. Amir, his girlfriend Marisol, and her mother, Teresa, came to the airport to welcome us. I had never met Marisol, nor seen her photo. Once we got out of customs, I looked around and saw Amir along with a beautiful young girl with long black hair, and her mother, waving hands. Amir came forward. We hugged and kissed. He then introduced us to Marisol and Teresa. They were lovely. From the beginning I felt they were family. They took us to their home for lunch, then on to a refugee hostel in Springvale. We stayed there for six months before renting a house.

I have faced many challenges during the last 30 years since arriving in Australia. I have achieved a lot in my life, building my life from nothing. I studied for five years at university, then started working for different companies as an accountant. After 16 years of work for other companies, I resigned and started my own business. Now I am a tax agent and my business is progressing rapidly.

I am a single and happy woman. Life has taught me a lot. I try to enjoy life in the best possible way! I believe in the Law of Attraction! I have learned not to give up hope!

Printed in Australia
AUHW022051040422
361844AU00002B/2

9 781922 691231